CEDE NULLIS

The author in 1944 before he went to OCTU.

Cede Nullis

A Personal History of the 1940 Normandy Campaign

Don Clark
4691882

The Pentland Press
Edinburgh – Cambridge – Durham – USA

First published in 2000 by
The Pentland Press Ltd,
1 Hutton Close,
South Church,
Bishop Auckland,
Durham

ISBN 1-85821-817-9

Typeset by Carnegie Publishing,
Carnegie House,
Chatsworth Road,
Lancaster

Printed and bound by Antony Rowe,
Chippenham, Wiltshire

British Library Cataloguing in Publication Data.
A catalogue record for this book is available
from the British Library

'*Cede Nullis*' is the Latin motto of KOYLI who were
formed in 1755 as the 51st Foot, and means
'Yield to None' or 'No Surrender'.

Contents

Illustrations

Dedication

I DEDICATE THIS STORY to my late friend Geoffrey Grimshaw whom I first met when I came to live at Wakefield Crescent, Earlsheaton, from Willans Road, Dewsbury Moor, in 1928. Geoffrey and I were then eight years old.

He and I grew up together, as playmates, school friends and young men with ideals, joining the Territorial Army at the end of 1938.

We went into the 1/4th Battalion KOYLI which was our local Regiment, went to camp in the summer of 1939, a camp on the Isle of Man, and thoroughly enjoyed it.

Two weeks later war was declared and those harmless little games in the 'Terriers' were no more. We were no longer 'Saturday night soldiers'.

Not long after mobilisation, the Army decided to create two battalions from one by splitting the 1/4th into two halves, and then later reinforcing each half with about 300 men. The new battalion was christened the 2/4th Battalion and it was to this that Geoff and I were assigned. This half of a battalion was then reinforced with 300 or so recalled regular army KOYLI reservists who had served in India and Afghanistan before the War in the late 1930s.

We, now a full strength infantry battalion of over 600 men, then went to France while the 1/4th Battalion, with our old Territorial friends, went to Norway.

The reinforcements for our battalion had alarming stories to tell about warfare against the Pathans and Afghans in the hills on the frontier between India and Afghanistan, of ghostly black dogs at night overrunning machine-gun posts and other strange incidents.

So the 2/4th Battalion, when we were sent to France in early 1940, comprised about 300 Territorials, about 100 reservists who had been demobbed in early 1939 after several years service in India, and about 250 transferees from the regular Indian Army. We were a mixed bunch and the men from India were a hard lot; I suppose the Top Brass reckoned they would stiffen us up!

This then was the outfit to which Geoffrey and I belonged and we had quite an exciting time with these regulars, hearing their stories and learning their drinking songs, particularly one about Queen Victoria and the camp followers in India.

Following the War, Geoff and I remained friends for the rest of our lives, both of us going into coal mining, starting in the NCB and then moving into engineering employment associated with mining. Geoff often called at our house in Cumbria when he could, and I called on him at Lowdham on those rare occasions when I was in Nottinghamshire.

The last time we met was in 1987 when Geoffry and Kate, his wife, spent a few happy days with us at our new home in Poole, Dorset. Not long after he died, so ours really was a lifelong friendship.

I still miss him, he would have been a good proofreader of this story had he lived longer – he was a good friend and we had a lot in common.

Foreword

WHILE THERE IS continuing interest in the Dunkirk evacuation of May 1940 we should also consider what was happening to the British Expeditionary Forces separated from the evacuation area by the successful German Forces. This part of the BEF was cut off from much of its command structure and was temporarily left to its own devices.

One such formation was the remains of the author's battalion, the 2/4th KOYLI, which had been largely destroyed by air attack north of Abbeville along with other units of the 46th Infantry Division. The author describes the events leading up to this and its aftermath, their subsequent fate as he knew it and the scrambled evacuation from France after the sinking of the *Lancastria.* He shows all the attributes of KOYLI fortitude, not forgetting how frequently they helped French refugees after they had been attacked by the Luftwaffe.

I recommend this account to everyone interested in the sad and largely overlooked events of this time, particularly the experiences of this young Territorial soldier.

There was a sudden realisation that the previously entertained hopes of this combined British Expeditionary Forces and French Forces, aided by those of Holland and Belgium, would be able to stop the advancing German armies as they did in 1914, became a myth. This was the same time Allied reinforcements from Normandy and the west were being destroyed by the enemy.

Survivors of these attacks were having to retreat west via Rouen, crossing the River Seine and delaying the enemy as best they could.

Don Clark shows how this was done, defending and helping civilians wherever possible, shooting up the enemy whenever he appeared and helping in the defence of Rouen. This went on for four weeks until they reached the Atlantic, culminating in an escape to England by a small tramp steamer, after the sinking of the evacuation liner *Lancastria* on 17 June 1940 north of St Nazaire.

He returned to his home in Dewsbury on 29 June 1940 via Plymouth, Mansfield and Sheffield having done all he could to obey the Regimental motto of 'Cede Nullis' – or 'Yield to None'.

Major C. M. J. Deedes
Regimental Secretary
King's Own Yorkshire Light Infantry

Preface

I THINK I MUST SAY what caused me to write this account of events happening so long ago and then inflict it on my family.

My son Nigel wanted me to write it – and by providing me with a word processor of sorts and assisted by my youngest son Adrian, who obtained a used printer for me, thrown out from Glory Mill where he worked, made it all possible. The word processor revived my limited typing skills, lost, I thought, when I left my clerical job with the RQMS of 2/4th Battalion KOYLI in early 1940 for the glamour of the Intelligence Section with Lieutenant Lee. Without the word processor my story would never have been written because I couldn't type on an ordinary typewriter in 1996 – I would have spent all my time erasing mistakes!

I also wanted to write it because I had found great difficulty over many years in getting any record of events in France in 1940 written by ordinary soldiers like myself. I visited the war museums at Cherbourg and Caen several times, and went to the Army Museum in Paris alongside Napoleon's tomb, but nowhere could I find anything significant.

I spoke with museum staff and consulted libraries but continued to be unsuccessful, so I decided that one day I would write my own account. It wasn't until 1994 when I was on holiday in my favourite part of France, at Perpignan, in the far south-west, that I was able to buy, at a discount, a French book on the subject which re-awoke my interest. The book was *Les Soldats de 40, dans la premiere Bataille de Normandie* written by R.G. Nobecourt, who says on the cover –

and I will translate the relevant part to English, and quote it because I think it is a very important statement:

'Much has been written on the battle of Normandy of 1944. But what a silence there is on that of 1940! That battle had about 2,000,000 victims who could not be blamed for their misfortunes.'

Nobecourt then goes on to say that he intends to write about La Bresle, Pays de Caux, the bridges over the Seine, the forest at Rouen and so on. All were places where I had been at this time in 1940, i.e. at the time of the First battle of Normandy referred to by Nobecourt which took place long after Dunkirk was over and done with.

I said I had found it almost impossible to find any writings on the subject and here was a famous French author, Nobecourt, saying the very same thing. And he was far better placed than I to research the literature for he was a professional.

So I had to write my story, though I hadn't been too enthusiastic about the thought of writing it in longhand for over forty years. Then Nigel spoke of his wish to see me write it and already had begun to seek out a used word processor for me to use. Now I had no choice, no excuse and consequently I began writing.

The old Tandem machine he obtained proved to be a marvellous tool for me, a heavy-handed mining engineer, so now here we are, the story is finished and I leave it to you, the reader, to decide if my labours have been worthwhile.

Acknowledgements

Finally, I must pay tribute to Madame Jacqueline Legrand of Abbeville who was born there long ago, has lived there all her life, and who was a tremendous help to me with her photographs of the city of Abbeville after the bombing of 20–21 May 1940.

Thank you Madame Legrand,
most sincerely,
Don Clark

Introduction

IT HAS BEEN SUGGESTED that I should write an introduction to the story of my life in the KOYLI, explaining generally my upbringing, my army training and so on that enabled me to behave as I did in the trying circumstances of Normandy, 1940.

My father was a First World War volunteer who joined up in early 1915 in a Hussar regiment – he loved horses and swords! His elder brother, who also joined up at about the same time from the telephone service of London, enrolled in the Army Signals of the day. He was only a private soldier but as a result of his London experience he was in truth a telephone wiring expert. He decided a job in signals would be a safer job for his younger brother than in the Hussars, no matter how dashing they appeared, and so, as was his right as an elder brother, he claimed my father into the signals, under what my father called 'the buddy system', or some such title.

My father left the Hussars and his sword, with which I believe he had become quite fond and very proficient, and became a signals wireman, with a pair of pliers and a roll of tape, on the Western Front, instead of a cavalryman in Mesopotamia, and served there throughout the War. During his service he was badly gassed twice, was demobbed in 1919, and after a poor record of health as a civilian finally died in 1933.

My mother was an Edwardian schoolteacher, who continued teaching throughout the War until my father came home to be demobbed. They initially lived in my mother's home in Manchester with her father, a widower, and her younger sister Hilda. Her younger brother George, a soldier in the Black Watch, was killed in France in 1917 while her elder brother, Edward, died during the War of a tropical fever in West Africa. Her mother also died about this time so her family was more than cut in half in these few war years and her husband was turned into an invalid. She always said she had nothing to thank the War for.

I was born in 1920 and had a good childhood with my father who invariably took me with him whenever he could. When I was eight or nine he took me in hand to teach me to box and to have some of the finer points of boxing imparted to me by one of his knowledgeable friends. This was done in order to instill in me the elements of self-defence and self-reliance. He ensured that when I went to Dewsbury Grammar School, aged eleven, I joined the Army Cadet Force. He was proud of this type of life and did not want me to be a 'softy' or be put upon. He wanted me stand up to aggressors, and to stop bullying wherever I met it. This I did on numerous occasions, sometimes at considerable cost to myself. When I got into a fight, a fist fight, and was beaten, as I sometimes was, he would be sympathetic, a case of 'Better luck next time, son, and you should do this and do that.' But no trips by him to complain to the other boy's father. And if I was the winner he would be so pleased, so triumphant, he would probably give me a tanner, or six pence, in old money.

His death was a shock to me and our family even though Mother had half expected it for many years. I was thirteen years old then, the eldest of a family of four children with the youngest being my baby brother of about eighteen months. It was 1933 and things were very difficult for us until I was old enough to leave the Grammar School prematurely and get a job as an apprentice mechanical engineer in early 1935. Shortly after that Mother got a job too, with the local authority for Dewsbury as a Children's Officer, a new job created for the welfare of children. So at last we were moving up, and life became a little easier financially.

I still maintained my keep-fit outlook on life, doing much cycling and camping on pre-war camp sites in outlying farmer's fields near such places as Scarborough, Bridlington, York and Knaresborough. When I got the chance I joined the Territorial Army, in the King's Own Yorkshire Light Infantry, 1/4th Battalion, the real army now, not, with all due respect, the Army Cadet Force.

Joining was quite an experience. I am not really sure when it was, either late 1938 or early 1939 when a squadron of the new caterpillar tracked Bren carriers, designed to carry infantry into battle with their Bren light machine-guns and ammunition, came into Dewsbury market place on a recruiting drive for the enlarged Territorial Army. They were the armoured personnel carriers of the day, very fast, very manoeuvrable and in Dewsbury that day, very glamorous! We virile male teenagers were bowled over by the sight of them, their power and speed and our minds filled with dreams that we were actually driving them. It was no contest, we would definitely join up and get a baby tank, although I must admit that it was a long time before we had our first driving lessons in Bren carriers such as these.

We were all fed up too by what we had read of Hitler and his Germany and were keen to do our bit so we – me and my mates – were there to join up along with a lot of other local lads. There were many of my long-standing friends there, all excited by this visit – Geoffrey Grimshaw, Stanley Hirst, Walter Petty among them. We were keen and enthusiastic, young, and maybe daft, but we wanted to offer our services. My mother certainly thought I was daft to follow the example of my father in being a volunteer, knowing how my father suffered and how he died as a direct result of joining up. But I wanted to be in and that was that. Only one of my close friends did not join with us, I don't know why that was, maybe his mother had more influence with him than mine had with me, but I never asked him.

I cannot remember all the details of the later signing-on ceremony but it was carried out one Sunday morning in Dewsbury drill hall on a trestle table covered with a grey army blanket. There was a bible on the table over which we swore allegiance to our sovereign, King George VI, all carried out before the Commanding Officer with the Adjutant and the RSM in attendance. It was very impressive and we received our 'King's shilling' from the Adjutant. After it was over we all retired to the bar in the drill hall where we recruits celebrated our new official status as Territorials, with drinks paid for by the CSM. An interesting sideline in this was that our allegiance was sworn to the King, and not to the Government or the Prime Minister. The King was our Commander-in-Chief and to reinforce this there were some symbols of royalty, such as the union flag, in the ceremonial accoutrements round the table.

There was also a strict medical, before the signing-on ceremony and of course we had attended many weekends on probation with the Terriers before we were accepted by them.

All this was in early 1939, as I remember it, long before any government announcement was made about conscription etc. That came later with all the new rules about reserved occupations though they were too late to stop me, even though as an apprentice designer toolmaker I was in a most critical reserved occupation – but that could not stop me as I was already in the Terriers as a fully signed-up member!

We quickly got our new battledress uniforms and field service caps – forage caps, we called them – shortly after joining in early 1939. I even had ample time before war was declared to order my made-to-measure dress uniform in dark barathea and to walk out in it round Dewsbury with the greatest pride. It cost me about two weeks civilian wages, a lot of money.

Strangely enough there was a shortage of military greatcoats and we had to wait several weeks even after war was declared before we got them. Meanwhile we made do with our civilian overcoats for which we were paid 6d per day, and what fools we felt wearing a mixture of khaki battledress with civvy overcoats. To minimise this we went out without coats, or in groundsheets if it rained.

In late July/early August we went on our one and only pre-war camp, to the Isle of Man for two clear weeks, or so we thought, but it turned out to be longer than that for many of us, including me, as we were kept on in the Army right up to the outbreak of war on 3 September, and after that we were in permanently!

The big event during this time at the camp was training and rehearsing for a very big parade which had not been done for a long long time. It was a divisional march past of nine infantry battalions, the cutting edge of the 49th Territorial Infantry Division, with the salute taken by our Major General. After about four days' rehearsal it went off perfectly, the bugle calls, bawling sergeant majors and nine blocks each of about 600 men per battalion in columns of three, split up into the five companies forming a battalion. We marched past the Divisional Commander, the Major General, standing at the salute at the front of his dais beneath its awning, at the high speed of light infantry, 140 paces per minute in perfect formation. The nine battalion blocks passed the saluting dais in three groups of three, each group being a brigade. I remember as if it were yesterday, our Brigade Sergeant Major screaming '135 Infantry Brigade – Eyes – Right' and we all saluted as we passed the dais with our rifles at the slope on our left shoulders. These men, yelling their orders, must have had lungs like elephants.

Each of the brigades were led by their brigadier with his sword raised in salute to the Major General and each of the nine battalion blocks were led by their colonels, also with their swords raised. It was a most stirring sight with almost the entire population of the Isle of Man with their Governor-General and the town council of Douglas watching it all in admiration.

I doubt if there had ever been a display like this on the island for centuries. It certainly went down a treat with we participants, even with all the attendant cleaning, polishing and blancoing. Despite what some modern-day critics may say about the futility of some army drill, this parade and its rehearsals came as a kind of pièce de résistance to all our previous weeks and months of infantry drilling and training. It was well worthwhile, and I think I speak for everyone there when I say we enjoyed it and were proud of our achievements that day.

The Sunday when war was declared, by default as it were, found us living in the drill hall at Dewsbury where we had been since we returned from the Isle of Man camp in early August. Some of the local married men had been sent home on our return but the majority of us new young single recruits stayed mobilised and the time was spent on continuing our training. So it was a useful period for us.

On that Sunday morning, 3 September, all the men were on parade in the drill hall, about 200 of us forming the full strength HQ Company of the Battalion, with the RSM, the Commanding Officer and the Adjutant in attendance, waiting to hear a radio broadcast by the then Prime Minister, Neville Chamberlain.

At 1200 hrs, noon, he spoke his very famous words 'and as no reply has been received at this time from Herr Hitler a state of war now exists between this counry and Germany' – and so we were at war. The officers on this parade retired to the Officer's Mess, presumably for a few stiff drinks, while the RSM, in all his finery, addressed we other ranks with these equally famous words, for us never to be forgotten: 'Attention, you men, you are no longer Saturday night soldiers, you are in the bloody Regular Army now, or you will be when the state of war has been promulgated this afternoon, and then we'll see what you're made of.'

And that was our introduction to the regulars and the beginning of a whole new way of life for us.

Following this, and the events of the day, we stayed at Dewsbury drill hall for several weeks, having our meals at a café in the town, drilling, marching, doing physical training, paying a visit to the firing ranges, mounting 24-hour guards at various strategic sites around town, doing forced marches and so on. I even think some of us had driving lessons on the carriers, though I wasn't given this honour. Much of this was hard work, particularly the 24-hour guards when we were on duty walking the area all through the night.

In late October 1939, I think it was, as certainly the war had been on for some months, a big change took place when the Battalion was split in two and the two halves were each eventually reinforced by about 300 men, thereby creating two battalions out of one. These reinforcements were a mixture of recalled Class A reservists, who had only just been released from the Regular Army after completing their years of service in India, and other men recalled direct to England from active service against Pathan tribesmen in areas of rebellion in Afganistan/Northern India. The split was made, as I remember it, by the simple system of parading us in ranks of three, there being about sixty such ranks for us in HQ Company. The front men of each rank numbered off in the usual manner, one, two, three, four, five etc. to sixty or whatever it was. The command was then given – 'even numbers stand fast, odd numbers quick march – left, right, left, right, right wheel' and off the parade ground. The even numbers, which included me and my pal Geoff Grimshaw stood fast as the others marched away. In due course we who had stood fast were transferred to the new battalion, now called the 2/4th Battalion KOYLI. We remained at Dewsbury for a few more days, feeling a bit lost now so many of our old mates were gone.

The others from the odd-numbered ranks who had marched away remained in the old battalion, the 1/4th, including our close pals Stanley Hirst and Walter Petty. They went to Strensall Barracks, York, where they were reinforced by another 300 or so men, like us. After much training in the next few months they went rather unexpectedly to the catastrophe of Norway in early 1940, instead of going to France like we did, where they suffered intense hardships and casualties in the fighting retreat to Narvik and were subsequently evacuated to Iceland.

Changes to battalions like this cause immense problems, dislocation of platoons, sections, mix-ups in administration staff and so on, though I do believe some share out of the existing key staff was pre-arranged so that on the whole things were not too bad. I got a good job out of it, after we moved from Dewsbury to Wakefield, to take over the now empty drill hall there, the job being that of a clerk assisting the RQMS with the daily ration indents for food for the five companies of the Battalion – vegetables, meat, bread, sweet stuff etc. I shared an office with a married soldier called Preston, recently recalled after completing his five years service in the Regular Army, mainly in India. He had married during his service to an English girl, though he had not seen much of her as most of his time had been spent in India. Nevertheless they had a baby about two years old, so he wasn't too pleased at being recalled so quickly to the colours again and leaving his family.

I remember we slept on a great big pile of army blankets in front of a blazing fire in the Quartermaster's stores, the fire being to keep the stores dry in the hard wet winter we were going through in South Yorkshire. We made toast in front of the fire for a late supper after we'd had a big evening meal down with our fellow QM workers in the cookhouse. This was a special meal, the raw materials, such as great slices of braised steak, being provided by our contacts at the Command Stores where our trucks went daily with our ration indents. It was a great life while it lasted.

After a few weeks the Commanding Officer, Lieutenant Colonel Hodgekinson, found out somehow, God knows how, that I was an engineering draughtsman, fairly skilled in blacksmithing, pipe work, hydraulics, steel frame works etc. – he had a big job for me, he said! He put me on a special task to prepare working drawings from a series of sketches and photos of military-style ablutions, urinals, water closets, cookhouse equipment and so on for the whole of the Battalion. These were to be what we now know as 'flat pack' –

designed to bolt together for quick assembly to water supplies and to be equally quickly dismantled for transport to a new site and used again. He had me installed in a surveyor's drawing office next door to the drill hall in Wakefield, where I worked away, twelve hours per day, seven days per week, for the three or four weeks needed to complete this urgent job in order to get badly needed facilities made for our men at all the various drill halls.

As soon as this task was completed I was put to work with our new RSM who was arranging basic accommodation for the great numbers of reinforcements joining us from the tribal warfare in India, having been posted back to England. This work involved me in measuring up all the rooms on the several floors of hotels, big houses and similar buildings in the centre of Wakefield, requisitioned by the Army for these men. I made floor plans of these buildings, printed copies of the plans in the surveyor's office and issued them to all concerned along with the RSM's comments about numbers of men per room, NCOs' rooms and so on. It was a big job, done under pressure, as the bed space allocations were urgently needed.

The CO, Lieutenant Colonel Hodgekinson, was delighted with all this. I think he was pleased he hadn't needed to call in the Royal Engineers for his various jobs, but all he gave me for it on completion was a week's leave – and no promotion!

After this, and by now we were into early 1940, I decided I had better get fit again, so I got out of my earlier job as a clerk and went back to ordinary soldiering. Later, when the Battalion Intelligence Section formed, the RSM put me into it as he reckoned they would find me useful for mapping duties.

And there I stayed, serving under Lieutenant Lee, going on a few minor courses on mapping work in the time remaining before we set off for France. Events there of course form the main story in this autobiography so I'll not repeat them here.

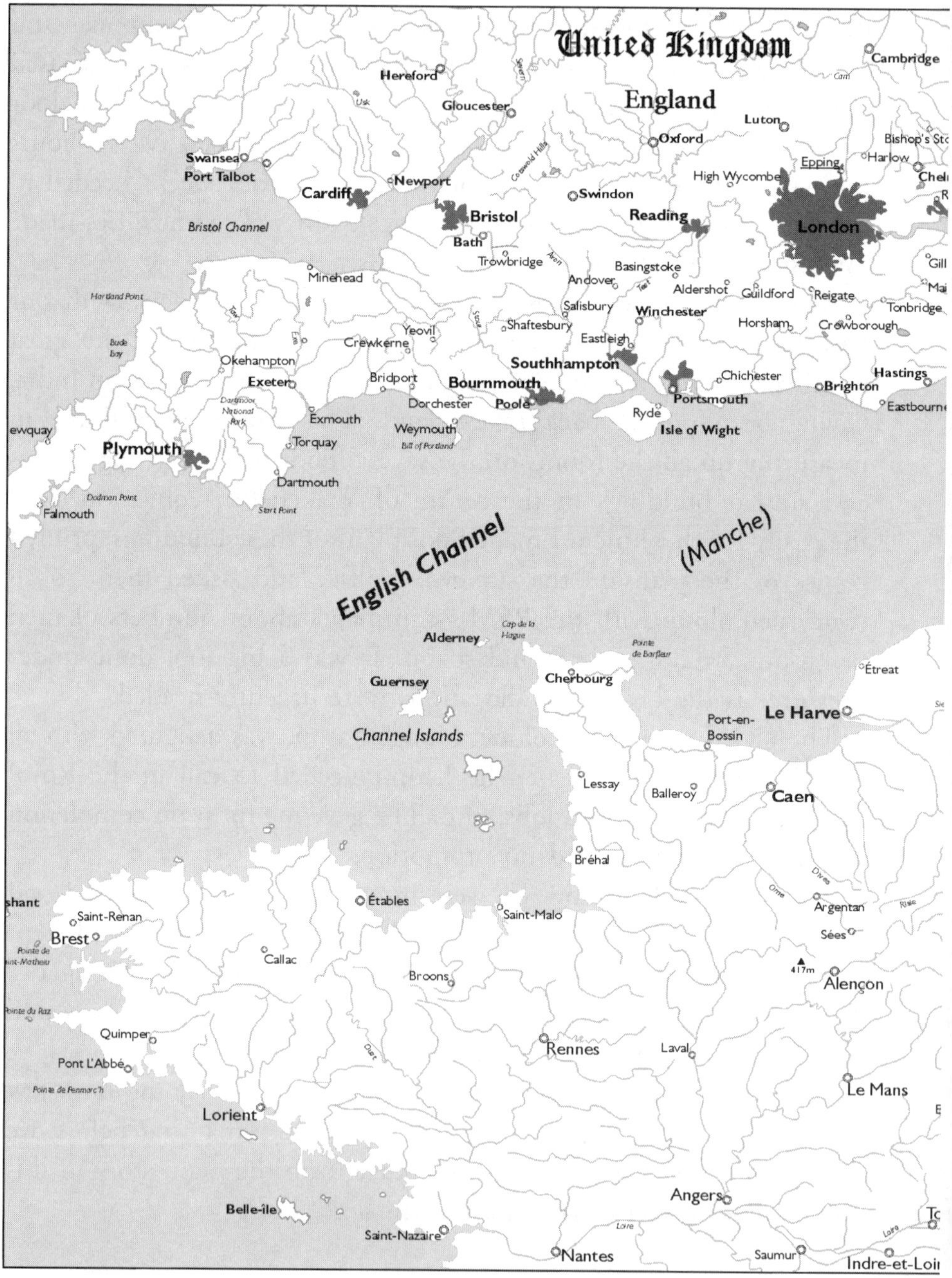

Southern England and NW France

NE France and Belgium

Chapter I

Moving from Rennes to North-Eastern France by Train

THE INVASION of the Low Countries by the Germans began in the early morning of Friday, 10 May 1940 in beautiful weather as the Allied armies moved forward in response to this attack by taking up prepared positions in Belgium.

At this time, we, 2/4th Battalion KOYLI, 46th Division, had been in France about four weeks and were camped at Tanouarn, about 30 km north of Rennes in Brittany. Many of the Battalion, those who I suspect were fully trained regular soldiers recalled from India to reinforce us – had been working on the nearby railway though some young soldiers, including myself, were continuously training for various new (to us) military tasks and skills, such as driving Bren carriers, firing the Bren LMG, firing the Vickers heavy machine-gun, curing stoppages on the machine-guns and map-reading work. We were also doing a lot of physical exercise, drill and bayonet practice as, believe it or not, it seemed to be expected by our commanders that we would be engaged in real hand-to-hand fighting with long steel bayonets in First World War style. This would be extremely bloody if it ever happened as we were taught to go for three critical soft spots on the body – the throat, up under the heart/lungs and in the lower abdomen!

For this bayonet practice, and with enormous exertion and rousing cries and screams, we used lifelike straw dummies, hanging in heavy wooden frames to support them against the impact of the bayonet and the swinging blows of the rifle butt in the follow-up attack. I found the bayonet often got stuck in the straw and hessian figure; when this happened it wasn't possible to belt the dummy across the head with the butt and so one felt one was rather inadequate.

The dummy, shaped like a man, was stiffened up with pieces of wood, and turnips, inside the straw to make it more lifelike. It was even said that some dummies were made more lifelike still by putting lumps of beef inside them so that the sticking effect of the bayonet was more realistic. I couldn't believe this story – to me it seemed that the lumps of beef would surely start to smell after a few days use in hot weather and quickly become unusable!

This 'sticking' effect in real live bodies was nevertheless confirmed by our Corporal Instructor, a First World War man, who had experienced real bayonet fighting on the Western Front in the last war. He warned us that if you went in the solid bony ribs of an enemy with the bayonet instead of in the soft area just under the ribs, it could get stuck there among the bones and the rest of it. So, he said, don't forget the three soft spots and go for them. To guard against getting my bayonet stuck like this I resolved then and there to always ensure I had a round up the spout if we went bayonet fighting so that I could blow my way out if the bayonet got stuck. It sounds dreadful I know, reading this now, but at the time in 1940, being aware of what is involved in war at close quarters and being prepared for it could save lives.

We didn't know then that the enemy front-line troops would attack with grenades and sub–machine guns, not bayonets and high-pitched screams, and later we heard stories that when the Highland Light Infantry went into a bayonet attack against German infantry from Saxony they were cut to ribbons before they ever got near the enemy firing their personal weapons, which were Schmeisser machine pistols. Our informant spoke with dismay of great big braw Scots lads, over 6 feet tall and 14 stone, being cut down by very average and mediocre lads from Hamburg whom he called 'brothel keepers and pimps'! It brought back memories for him of the Scots with their broadswords, kilts and courage being blown away by the Hanovarian/English redcoats and their cannon fire at Culloden.

If you must condemn anything, after reading this account of some aspects of our training, condemn war and the politicians who dabble in it with their treaties, protocols etc. and the press with their general sanitising of it. They seem to be unconcerned at the inevitable bloody consequences for those involved at the real cutting edge, like the infantry.

Thank God, sincerely, we never experienced this type of hand-to-hand warfare and I was never to suffer any trouble with my conscience if I had had to inflict terrible wounds with a bayonet. Somehow, killing or trying to kill via a bullet at a range of 200 to 300 yards seems cleaner, even though the end result for the enemy is the same.

Although the real war had started on 10 May, we knew little at the time about the detail of the events. There was no censorship, but equally there was no news and so we were somewhat in the dark as to what was happening on the other side of France. We knew the Allied armies had moved forward very quickly into Belgium as planned, and we knew that in the normal course of events we would move forward behind them to take up the positions they had left, so we expected to follow them very soon. But we had been kept waiting to move for nearly a week, and we'd had our special pay parade when we got two weeks pay, say 200 francs each on average (1939) to keep us going, but we were still waiting.

Meanwhile we were kept hard training during all the hours of daylight, seven days a week – and fortunately the weather stayed sunny and warm. Had it rained, with us under canvas, it would have been murder. The machine-gun training was the most enjoyable for me – apart from firing the guns we were taught how to clean them, clear stoppages, set them up for firing and so on. We even practised these skills in the dark by being blindfolded.

Grenade throwing was also carried out from dugouts representing trenches, instructors even drilling us in how to pick up live grenades from the floor, from the mud, to throw back at the enemy before they exploded under you. Give them back his own, the instructor said, do it slowly, no rush, no bloody heroes, and don't let it slip in your hand! Count slowly, in seconds, one er – bend down, two er – pick it up, three er – throw and four, quick – duck down!

He would tell us that grenades had either a four-second delay or a seven-second delay. If it was four seconds, you would be dead anyway, as you had no chance regardless of whether you tried to pick it up or not, it would either explode in your hand or else explode in the air in front of you. But if it was a seven-second grenade you would be OK, although your enemy would be dead. Oh yes, it was all very exciting and dangerous but would be most useful no doubt.

The Battalion came to France in mid-April, from Southampton to Cherbourg, on the Isle of Man boat *Tynwald*, leaving early in the morning with an escort of three destroyers. I don't know how many men were on board the *Tynwald*, probably 2,000 in all, but there were too many and so volunteers were asked for to travel on the destroyers. I and maybe 100 others stepped forward and were distributed on the three escorts and I found myself on the destroyer H33, HMS *Vanoc*, standing on the open deck near the stern. It was a lovely sunny day, the sea was calm and we moved along nice and smoothly, positioned on the port side of the *Tynwald*.

After some hours sailing, and when the wind had become sufficiently chilling to cause me to seek shelter from it down a companionway to warm up, we suddenly came to action stations with much hooting on the klaxons. The next thing I was aware of was that the ship came up to full speed, probably 40 knots, swung away in a big semicircle, swerving tightly later and heeling over with the speed, coming back on itself to attack what was obviously a German U-boat with a barrage of depth charges. The other two escorts joined in the attack with us, taking our place as we moved away from the area of the U-boat to be nearer the *Tynwald.* Together then we two went as fast as possible towards Cherbourg, leaving the other two escorts to deal with the U-boat. It was a few minutes of high drama and excitement, the thrill of which did not leave me until we went through the outer wall of Cherbourg harbour, past the forts, into relative safety.

After disembarking in mid-afternoon we were given a haversack ration and time off in Cherbourg town with strict orders to be at the railway station by 2200 hrs. For most of us this was our first visit to France and we made the most of it! Some, the older ones mainly, went to the brothels; a few, a minority I have to say, went to see the sights of the town, the harbour, the shops, and sent cards back home to their wives and girlfriends. Most of us sat on the quay to eat our rations in the sunshine, looking at the boats, which was how I knew the destroyer on which I had sailed was H33. I could see these enormous unforgettable numbers on the side of the ship, just forward of the funnel, from where I was sat, before we eventually went off to find some excitement in the bars of the Old Town behind the harbour.

And excitement we did find; I and my mates met up with a party of 'Jocks' who had come in on another boat a few hours earlier. They were wearing the kilt and this caused no end of ribald comments from French sailors we met up with during our later pub crawl. As we became more and more inebriated fights broke out in the street as the sailors wanted to see what the 'Jocks' were wearing under the kilt! Then the gendarmes came with their rolled macs which they used very effectively as clubs to subdue the worst of the drunks; next came the French redcaps, and finally the British redcaps. It began to look nasty and so I and a few of my mates ducked out through the back door of the bar we were in, to avoid the police in the street, and to make our way round to the railway station. As I ran out and down the back lane I heard the big bangs of exploding 'thunderflashes' as some of the 'Jocks' became goaded beyond endurance by the redcaps and the 'frenchies' and decided to make a real fight of it. It was like the 1812 Overture, a real send-off!

And so we got to our train, which was fairly comfortable, rather like pre-war 3rd class Southern Railway stock, and set off at midnight on our journey into the unknown. Later the next day we found ourselves at Rennes – but where was Rennes ? We later discovered it was in Brittany, some 200 miles south-west of Cherbourg and there we stayed for nearly a month training frantically to get us battle fit.

So, since arriving in France we had been training every day all the hours of daylight, seven days a week except for one weekend when we went to Rennes for twenty-four hours of wildness, women and booze. That was something to remember and tell your grandchildren about, oh yes indeed, though I haven't wanted to do so yet! It was one of those events which cements morale and camaraderie among soldiers. I still remember coming back to camp in the rear of an army troop transporter, with my mates – Innis, the handsome lad whose name I forget who had a pretty sister, Preston and others – leaning out of the truck, hanging on to the tubular steel canopy frames, singing our heads off and showing our souvenirs of the night out to one another.

One event I can refer to was when a few of us had come out of the forces club and were standing in the middle of one of the long sides of the big rectangular square in the centre of Rennes having a breath of fresh air. It was late at night, it had been raining and the cobblestones surfacing this square were wet and slippery. We were having a smoke under an awning when a Citroen car came into the square from one of the far top roads on our right at high speed. It was one of the very handsome black Citroens of the late 1930s, the 'traction avant', the type used by the police and Maigret in films. It was going so fast that we expected it to go straight across the end of the square and away. But no, incredibly, without making the slightest effort to slow down it suddenly turned right, at speed, to come down our side of the square towards us. In the midst of making the right turn it suddenly flipped over and made a complete revolution sideways while still moving forward, landed on its four wheels and in a shower of sparks, a scream of metal and a puff of exhaust smoke it was gone down the other corner on our left and out of sight missing us by a few feet!

Had we witnessed an escaping criminal or was it a police car in hot pursuit of someone? We never did find out so we made our way back into the club and the pleasures of the night.

Another great week was when the 'Army Bath Unit' came to camp with a small fleet of special lorries and we all had the luxury of a hot bath. That was a special treat, believe me, to be really clean again.

We had still not quite got over the fact that we were in a foreign country, using foreign money, talking foreign. It was all very strange to most of us who hadn't been further than Blackpool illuminations. I remember going down to the local estaminet, some two or three miles away, a *bierre* house/cafe called 'Le Coq d'Or'. And there I was telling the locals of the cost of living in northern England, about what my wages as an engineer would buy before I was called up in mid-August 1939 and of life generally in peacetime.

We also had a special church service in three parts for the C of Es, the RCs and the 'others'. In this army you could not be agnostic or atheist, you had to be one of these three. This service was an open-air drumhead service held on the Sunday a few days after the Germans invaded Belgium and was very moving and impressive.

Then suddenly, in the midst of this very active yet almost peaceful atmosphere, with its completely new kind of rural life, living under canvas in a big field, a spirit of sudden urgency seized the camp on Friday/Saturday, 17/18 May 1940.

The urgency was with the sudden packing by over 600 men of kit bags, stores of all types, weapons and ammunition as we got ready for what was obviously a major move. Fleets of lorries came to the camp, like those we experienced before when the whole battalion had been taken to Rennes for twenty-four hours of freedom, but this time they were loaded with stores instead of men. This was obviously to be a real move up to the frontal area near Belgium at long last and a serious matter for us as we were being taken away from what, rather surprisingly, had become our home from home. The likelihood now was of being pitched into inhospitable surroundings of violence. We'd even had a religious service to see us off!

It was therefore a time of great excitement when we were paraded as a full battalion of over 600 men, given our 48-hour haversack rations and eventually marched, cheered by the locals, to the station, or goods siding, at Montreuil-sur-Ille, near Tanouarn Camp, where we entrained with some Royal Engineers on the evening of 18 May 1940 for Rennes. From there we carried on to some further onward unknown destination, which we were later told was Arras, via Lisieux, Elboeuf, Rouen and Amiens. The train was a bit of a honky-tonk of old railway trucks marked '8 horses/40 men' but it had a powerful modern locomotive, seemingly bigger than those in England, having a wheel configuration of 4–8–2 or similar. There was also a funny old six-wheeled coach, probably from about 1870, set near the middle of the train for the use of the officers, RSM and HQ clerks, the sort of coach likely to have seats covered in old green velvet!

It rolled along, probably at a steady 20 or 30 miles an hour, on what seemed eventually to become minor tracks with grass growing between the sleepers or flat steel cross ties where there were no sleepers. Most of us fell asleep on the straw which covered the floor of these old wooden vans from the First World War when it really got dark, after eating some of our sandwiches and fruit in the haversack rations. The sliding doors were wide open because after the closeness of the night following what had been a hot day, we needed to get fresh air in. I suppose in a way it was comfortable enough and sleep came quickly to us young carefree soldiers.

After a few hours jogging along at this speed we slowed down to a comfortable walking pace, and inevitably some of the more restless blokes jumped off the train to have a quick 'Jimmy-Riddle' until they realised they could save energy by doing it out of the open doorways!

It was a pleasant enough journey through a balmy spring night crossing Brittany and Normandy, warm, starlit, uneventful and peaceable, and really most of us hadn't a care in the world.

There was one slight excitement in the middle of the night however when a young soldier went down with a severe pain in the guts. Somehow the OC Train and the Medical Officer must have got a message through to higher authority as in due course our train stopped at some unknown rural station or halt where incredibly an ambulance train of the Red Cross was waiting for us. It was all lights, red crosses on the sides and roofs, bags of activity, nurses in white starched uniforms and most amazing of all, the train comprised new maroon and cream LMS coaches. To us it was 'Home'. A great roar went up from all as we watched our colleague carried aboard on a stretcher – 'you lucky devil' some yelled. As the trains set off moving again, in opposite directions, we settled back to sleep on our straw on the hard wooden floor, somehow comforted by the thought of this super ambulance train, and all the others like it, for our use if we were wounded in the next few weeks, was on its way back to Cherbourg and England. Later we heard this lad had appendicitis, so it wasn't all beer and skittles for him though it got him back to his home and away from all the ups and downs that were to face us.

Meals turned out to be something of a problem – once we had eaten our haversack rations they were almost non-existent except for mess tins of tea given to us at stops every few hours, which enabled the cooks to brew up in dixies using boiling water from the locomotive. Breakfast on the second day, however, Sunday, 19 May 1940, was something of a feast, with tins of cold rolled American bacon, thick slabs of bread and butter and the inevitable cans of tea at the next halt.

It was a quiet day, slow moving and dull with lots of stops and starts, but by the evening we had got to Rouen, Sotteville, some twenty-four hours after leaving Rennes. We stopped there for a while with the locomotive puffing and blowing, which was said to be a halt to await fresh instructions. Eventually we got moving again and by early the next morning, on what was the third day, Monday, 20 May 1940, we had all fed and shaved early and were beginning to wonder where we were heading. We did hear on the 'grapevine' however that it was no longer to Arras, with some of the better informed thinking it could be St Pol or Bethune.

Wherever it was, it seemed to be taking a long time to get there and we were getting restless. Boredom, because we had nothing much to do, began to affect us a bit by now but the RSM with the CSMs sorted some of it out at the next stop when they posted more AA guards on the several trucks fitted with observation hatches. These were stout wooden structures on the roofs of the trucks fitted with Lewis guns – by building up the AA defences in this way and by generally giving us jobs to do cleaning the weapons, they kept us occupied. However, because of the enhanced AA precautions and the time we had spent on this journey so far, we knew we must by now be approaching a danger area – perhaps the fresh instructions at Rouen may have warned the OC Train of this.

I was one of those given a job on the enhanced AA guard, mainly, I think, because the CSM of HQ Coy knew me as a machine-gunner. It was a responsible job, watching out for enemy aircraft from behind a Lewis gun mounted on a bodged-up but solid enough mounting on top of one of these observation posts. They were rather like gigantic wooden chimney pots at the rear end of some of the trucks with a narrow steel ladder inside them. I thought manning a Lewis gun would be routine for me, a piece of cake really after all the training I had done – but I was soon due for a surprise! The train had not been running for much more than an hour, indeed I had barely time to get my eye in and fire off a few bursts to warm the gun when there was a sudden roar of aircraft engines and two shapes flashed past about fifty feet away above and to one side of the train. They came from out of the sun at the end of a dive, flashed along the length of the train firing at us then climbed away at a shallow angle and turned clockwise through nearly 360 degrees to attack us again. We could see the black Nazi crosses on the wings and fuselage, and when I saw these identification symbols my heart skipped a beat.

They were Messerschmitt fighters, 109Es, but we had difficulty seeing them because of the sun in our eyes, so I fired somewhat blindly forward off to the left-hand side a bit when I heard the noise of their engines again rising towards a crescendo, plus the noise of firing. Oddly enough the noise was not too loud until they were right on top of us. I fired in their direction along the train into the sun, at a low angle of elevation, hoping to hit them if they came again on the same line as before. The rest of the battalion, except for the AA guards, had jumped off the slow-moving train and were already running for cover towards a nearby wood to our left. The two aircraft struck the train again and this time bullets ripped through the side of the wooden trucks, missing me by about six feet. All this action took about ten seconds, indeed the last of our men had still not reached the wood with the RSM behind them hobbling on his walking stick as a result of a sprained ankle.

The Messerschmitts turned away and to our surprise were quickly lost to sight. Our mates from the wood came back, as soon as they heard the bugle sounding the recall, while we men on AA guard began to clean our guns and replace the pans of ammo. Roll calls were made and to our amazement not one out of over 600 men had been hurt – incredible! Some wisehead said later that the aircraft were probably low on ammo and did not want to use it all up on us in case they met the RAF.

This episode did have one useful result though – it made us very aware of the dangers and the need to keep alert. A short time later our train pulled into what was obviously the outskirts of a big town, which turned out to be Dieppe, Rouxmesnil Junction in fact, but what were we doing there? We were supposed to be heading for Abbeville or Amiens (according to the jungle telegraph) not Dieppe.

Rumour then had it that the cause of our diversion was sabotage, to delay us, like so many other delays and confusions being created in France at this time by German parachutists. They were said to be disguised as nuns or policemen and were believed to be able to take over and control traffic throughout the whole north-eastern area of France. Indeed some cynics said they could walk on water! Be that as it may, we were surely not intended to go to Dieppe because as a result of this diversion we had lost the best part of a day. And this was to have unforeseen dramatic results later.

However, we kept on rolling once we cleared Dieppe, without any more alarms, and by late that evening, 20 May 1940, we were approaching Abbeville. We slowed up as we neared the city and ran on into what seemed to be an enormous marshalling yard on the western side, stopping alongside another train like ours. As we pulled up their sliding doors opened and there were the 'Dirty Dukes', men of the Duke of Wellington's Regiment; in other trains on nearby tracks were Green Howards, Sherwood Foresters, East Lancs, and so it went on, train after train all stood in this great goods yard. There must have been seven or eight troop trains on parallel tracks, all waiting for something. There were other trains carrying vehicles, Bren carriers and so on. Perhaps at this point I should say that the famous 'Dirty Dukes' were neighbours of ours at home, being from the

Halifax area while we were from Dewsbury-Batley-Wakefield-Normanton, so we were fellow countymen of sorts.

But to resume, why were all these trains waiting here? There were troop trains, trains of flat cars carrying Bren carriers, 15-cwt trucks, 6-wheeler troop transports, 2-pdr anti-tank guns with limbers and quads – they were all there, it seemed to be all the tackle for a division. We could not see too much in the dark but it was obvious something big was going on which concerned us, so we waited impatiently for events to unfold.

We must have waited an hour or so, it was now nearly midnight, and the only light was that given out by the locomotive fire boxes whose red gleam illuminated the track under them and the glowing ends of thousands of cigarettes. Then at long last, one of the troop trains began to move forward, slowly, towards the eastern exit from the yard. It was as if a log jam had been broken and we were obviously on the move at last. Then suddenly, before we could savour our good fortune of being on the move again and going somewhere, all hell broke loose as with no warning, no sign of impending trouble, bombs rained down from what must have been fleets of bombers high overhead, whose engines we had not heard before because of the noise from the steam engines, clanking and hissing and spluttering.

We knew now we should have left this yard earlier, we had been held up too long, passing time talking to our mates, the 'Dirty Dukes' about the previous minor air attack near Dieppe and the alleged diversion to Dieppe when we were supposed to be going somewhere else in an easterly direction. In some way this little attack by Messerschmitts earlier on us KOYLIs gave us temporary status over the 'Dirty Dukes', but it had delayed us long enough to put us bang on target for this major strike by the Luftwaffe. Now we were all going to get more status than we ever bargained for!

Within seconds strings of bombs were exploding all round us, trains, trucks, vehicles and ammunition were on fire, exploding in all directions in great fireballs from the bombs, some obviously very big ones indeed. I saw men trying to unshackle the turnbuckles on Bren carriers and 15 cwts while all this was going on, though what they were going to do when they were unshackled heaven knows. There were no platforms or quays to run on to that I could see from our train so really it looked like work for nothing. I saw other men blown up in the fireballs of the explosions, a ghastly sight of bodies like twisted rag dolls going up in the air for maybe thirty feet. Others showed all the signs of bad injuries, such as severe burns, shrapnel wounds, blast, concussion and the rest. The regimental medics were rushed off their feet.

We tried to remove ammunition boxes full of .303 ammo from the wagons of our train – but on the whole it was wasted effort because the kitbags piled up in front of the boxes prevented us getting at them. We got some of the ammo boxes off, and Bren guns, but it was hopeless. God knows how many casualties there were in a matter of a few minutes but there must have been hundreds. A surprising thing in all this was that I did not see any panic or cracking of discipline. Troops stayed in the area doing what little they could to help their mates or salvage some equipment.

After a quarter of an hour or so of this one-sided carnage I and others were directed by some officers towards a small road leading to a bridge across a river or canal ahead of us. This must have been some distance away from the exploding trains, a scene which was by now like Dante's inferno, flame making it all seem as bright as day even though it was the middle of the night, with the crackle of exploding ammunition now dinning in our ears to spur us on if we needed any spurring. I began to appreciate more and more as I crossed the bridge, thereby putting some distance between myself and the destruction, that away from the smoke and explosions it was a clear, moonlit, starry night – all stars and a brilliant moon, not a cloud in the sky and if you looked away from the bombing and forgot for a moment what was happening back there, it seemed so very, very beautiful. The stars and their constellations were so brilliant and the sky so purple, it really was lovely.

So, after a few minutes of real BLITZKRIEG we were back to our basic format as light infantry. We were very light too, with no

Pont Laviers, a bridge we crossed to go North of Abbeville on 20/5/1940 and re-crossed to retreat to Abbeville town and the Dieppe direction on 21/5/1940

vehicles, little ammunition, no food and a bit disorganised. We were struggling individually or in small groups towards the east where we could just discern the dawn breaking. Our last order had been shouts to get to open country behind and to the north of the town of Abbeville and then form into small groups and wait for dawn before making our rendezvous with the regiments or battalions in this area.

It was now the beginning of what was to be a most fateful day for everybody in France – Tuesday, 21 May 1940.

Unknown to us, at this moment, because we were simply glad to be alive and in one piece in our little corner, a new super German army was bypassing us and the city of Abbeville on its north-east side. An army comprising several Panzer divisions, it was a Panzer Army, commanded and staffed, as we now know, by some of the finest and most experienced Panzer generals Hitler possessed: von Runstedt, Guderian, Hoth and Rommel, plus their staff officers and unit commanders. It was Rommel who was in command of the leading Panzer divisions which, on 21 May 1940, were sweeping up towards Arras and St Pol from this breakthrough and Hoth who had gone straight ahead with his Panzer divisions for the English Channel. He was now past Abbeville, on the northern side, and nearing the sea, about to sweep up the coast to the Channel ports of Le Touquet, Boulogne and Calais.

This Panzer Army, along with other similar armies, each comprising about 1,500 tanks with its own 700 or so close-support aircraft, 200,000 men, supplies of food, petrol and ammunition, all motorised, had burst through the Ardennes valleys, which were very passable because of the dry winter, crossed the River Meuse between Sedan and Mazieres after a short struggle and cut through the French Ninth Army.

The initial breakthrough was with two Panzer divisions, the point division commanded by Rommel, who struck at the junction of two French armies, the Second and the Ninth, the Second being on the northern side. This was a most alarming development, as it had not been foreseen, and von Runstedt made it infinitely worse for the Allies by reinforcing the success with another five or six Panzer divisions waiting in reserve, thereby creating what was in effect a super Panzer Army of enormous and unstoppable capability at that time. Rommel soon turned to the north behind Arras with two or three Panzer divisions while the other three or four Panzer divisions headed west for the coast prior to sweeping up through the channel ports.

The field command of this army was taken over by Guderian himself. This force then swept right across the rear of the Allied armies, cutting off their lines of communication to Paris and the south and west. Its leading armoured brigades were to pass north of Amiens and Abbeville on 21 May 1940, just as we reached the Abbeville area east of the Somme waterways after our near destruction in the marshalling yard west of the city. We in fact were struggling to rendezvous as individuals and small groups in the very area towards which this German Panzer Army was at this moment heading at full speed.

But we were in ignorance of these great events, as were most other people at this time. And so we were due to have an exciting meeting if we were not very careful, for if we didn't stop soon it would be our last meeting with anyone.

Chapter II

Moves Forward Beyond Abbeville on Foot and the Return

MOVEMENT TOWARDS THE BRIDGE and eventually crossing the river or canal quickly in the dark became something of a shambles, absolutely chaotic, tripping over the rails and sleepers despite the brilliant moonlight and the reinforcing starlight. In the red sky area behind us explosions were everywhere with shouting, casualties, the crackle of exploding ammunition, fires springing up and the noise of aircraft and the scream and detonation of bombs. After we had crossed the bridge, now illuminated by the fires and the multiple flashes of explosions, amid and despite all the confusion, we knew that going in the general direction away from the water was temporarily the only way to safety and to the supposed rendezvous behind Abbeville. Staying near the trains would be suicide and no use to anyone, so it was 'Go Go', get on, get away.

Events in the next few hours, up to dawn, and just after, are vague to me but I do know that come daylight some forty or fifty of us KOYLIs found ourselves lying on our groundsheets at the side of a hedge, dry, fairly comfortable but worn out as a result of the unaccustomed poor sleep and excitements we'd had in the last few days. I remember it as a small field, maybe three or four acres with some fruit trees, knarled somewhat, and we seemed to be behind a row of terraced houses on a road or street. A German fighter aircraft, whose Nazi crosses we could see clearly, flew low along this road but didn't see us, and we didn't move to draw his attention. We rested a few hours then, without any breakfast, because we had no food except the iron rations, got to our feet and set off to attempt to get well behind the town of Abbeville on to a road in the general direction of St Pol. Our party included the CSM of HQ Company, the Dewsbury chap who had been with us for over a year and whose name I now forget, the new RQMS, for whom I worked briefly at Wakefield before we came to France and a few of the junior officers. In charge of us was the Adjutant, Captain Keeping. So we were a fairly cohesive group, small but with more than our fair share of officers and senior NCOs. Somehow also, during this night of excitement, I had changed my rifle for a Bren light machine-gun with three full magazines. It was a good swop, I would say.

We moved in small groups of five or six, separated by perhaps 100 feet so as to ensure we were not trapped in a bunch, and got on what seemed to be a main road going north-east, judging by the sun, moving to it from the rear of our field and across neighbouring fields. To our surprise we found the road was congested with refugee traffic, both civilian and military, moving south-west back in the direction from which we had just come. The road was packed; it was incredible, I had never seen anything like it. There were horse-drawn farm carts piled high with household possessions pulled by tired-looking horses with children sat on wherever a space could be found and the adults pushing at the rear to help the horse; families with smaller carts with mattresses on top pulled by a donkey or a big dog like a St Bernard, and hand carts, wheelbarrows and prams taking all they could carry being pushed by other family members. It was unbelievable and we began to realise what war could really do and what war meant to civilians who had the misfortune to get in the way. There were a few cars of the wealthier people but they could only proceed at the walking speed of the multitude and then to top it all were the columns of thousands of walkers with suitcases

Refugees moving across the cross-roads in spite of the recent bombing

(Imperial War Museum F4507)

A small group just beginning their indefinate walk to what they hope is safety

(Imperial War Museum F4706)

Refugee lorry packed with all generations of a family

(Imperial War Museum F4715)

Top: *Farm vehicles joining the refugee column; all will then move at the same speed as the tired old horse*
(Imperial War Museum F4716)

Bottom: *Mixed Refugee columns with trucks, carts and walkers. A special target for enemy fighters*
(Imperial War Museum F4708)

and carrier bags. I say thousands of walkers, maybe tens of thousands or perhaps even hundreds of thousands.

It was an endless procession of misery and weariness and I found it astonishing and mindboggling to see so many people, adults and children, and animals, struggling to get away from something they obviously feared. I began to wonder what we were letting ourselves in for. It was so hot by now, even though it was only mid-morning, with that sun blazing down again out of a cloudless sky and us in our heavy uniforms and greatcoats plus a big pack on our backs. God, it was hot!

We moved off this road as quickly as we could to get away from these crowds, indeed I don't think we were on it for more than 200 or 300 yards before we were able to move off onto a minor side road which looked to be going generally in the same direction, i.e. towards the north-east, opposite to the way the crowds were walking. This road was quieter, though there were some walkers, and we thought we could make better speed in what we hoped would be the direction of St Pol without being blocked by the endless columns of carts and refugees. After we'd gone a mile or so on this back road and while we were having a breather in some back gardens in a very small hamlet of only a few houses, we saw two fighter aircraft dive down to machine-gun the columns of refugees we had just left. Their plan was obviously to harass the refugees, to shoot 'em up and keep them on the move. When they came down again, flying low past our front at an angle so as to intersect the main road somewhat obliquely prior to turning so as to fly along it at low level, we let rip with our several Bren guns firing from the hip. I don't know if we hit them but firing at an enemy certainly cheered us up and got the adrenalin flowing.

Going on, we joined a seemingly better class of road running downhill and twisting through the trees at the beginning of a forest, and came unexpectedly on the rear of an apparently abandoned gun position. This comprised two 75-mm field guns on solid steel wheels, the famous French 75s, well dug in behind sandbags and tree trunks, lots of ammunition in the limbers, well camouflaged and with several outlying protective machine-gun nests – but no gunners! As it seemed a good site for guns among the trees, on a winding road up a hill ready to ambush tanks or trucks as they came up and round a corner, probably in low gear, with the sun in their eyes if it were sunny and midday, we wondered why the guns were not manned. Strange they were abandoned, so maybe they were a fall-back position. But it had an unreal look about it, almost as if it were a mirage, a sort of 'Marie Celeste'. No men manning the guns, yet they were real killer guns as with the armour-piercing shells from the limbers they would make mincemeat out of the heaviest German tank of the day.

Not long after passing through this position, we heard the sound of artillery start up over towards Abbeville, perhaps ten miles away to the right, and after two or three more miles of marching in our open-order formation, we reached the edge of the forest we had been coming through without further incident. Somehow however, we felt we were now likely to come across enemy troops at any moment and consequently the open order formation was a wise precaution. The Adjutant must have thought the same about the dangers of German troops as now he decided to keep the main body of his few men under cover near the edge of the forest and send a small patrol forward, stripped of the heavy greatcoats and back packs, across the intervening open farmland to the top of a small ridge, perhaps another mile and a half away, to see what was happening far ahead.

So Lieutenant Lee, the regimental Intelligence Officer, with about four men including an NCO and myself, all of us members of the partially trained Intelligence Section formed back at Rennes, set off to reconnoitre whether it was safe for the main body to cross this stretch of fairly open farmland after leaving the safety of the wooded area. We had first to cross a rather narrow strip of trees and hedgerows which gave plenty of cover before going through an extensive area of mixed farmland with a few simple buildings and sheds. Then we reached the more open country far ahead using a broken hedge as initial cover. Before us, maybe another half a mile away, was our target, a low hill, rather long and elongated forming a ridge with large patches of shrubbery and gorse on the margins, and with a copse of a few trees on the brow of this ridge which blocked the view of the Adjutant who was further back. But when we got to the top of the ridge, after an uneventful mixture of running doubled up across the open stretches and ducking behind occasional hedges and trees, we found ourselves in a superb viewpoint with very good cover among the trees and bushes. We had a wonderful wide-ranging open view to both left and right and well forward, beyond where we lay, to what was a real main road, perhaps half a mile away. This road clearly ran from the Abbeville and Amiens area on the right towards the direction of the sea far away on the left. So the five of us settled down in the undergrowth and grass, got our binoculars out and slowly and carefully crept forward the few yards needed to get a really good clear open view of conditions ahead on this main road.

What a shock I got as I looked through the binoculars – I could see the main road in front of us was filled for the several miles in view with a non-stop stream of tanks, guns and motorised infantry moving from right to left with motorcycle outriders travelling up the sides of this enormous column.

It was a truly impressive sight, stretching as far as we could see to both the left and the right. They were doing about 20 miles per hour so that about 2,000 or so vehicles an hour were passing us. We observed this for maybe two or three hours, in the hope that the traffic might stop so we and the rest of our comrades could perhaps get behind the tail end of the column if we found the end and so cross the road in relative safety. But it went on and on, with occasionally a gap of only about 100 yards appearing in the column, presumably to cater for breakdowns by creating a chicane, and then it would continue, going on and on and on. There must have been several divisions, motorised and armoured moving across our front, and quite clearly there would be all the inevitable supply columns, food, petrol, medical etc. with all their escorting infantry. There was a pall of exhaust smoke hanging over the road with a continuous low roar from the thousands of engines. It seemed as if this traffic could in fact have been going on for hours, perhaps even for days, so after a few hours of observing it there didn't seem much point in staying there indefinitely once we were pretty sure the way ahead was blocked. There were also the occasional flights or squadrons of aircraft flying over the column, in both directions, possibly flying shotgun for all this traffic. So a dash across the enemy's line of advance by our small party of men would be suicide.

We returned to the main body and Lieutenant Lee reported to the Adjutant who sent another patrol back towards Abbeville. We, meanwhile, were given a snack of bread and bully beef, our first bite of the day, and told to rest while some of the others were put on guard. I don't know what went on with the patrol who went back to the Abbeville area the but the next thing I was aware of was that we were paraded and told orders were that we now had to get back to the Channel coast, to Dieppe or to some other small harbour beyond Dieppe to the west, moving in small groups so as to avoid air attack. There, hopefully, the Division would be reforming in some new command.

These were definite orders from our officers who must have received orders from somewhere further back, no euphemisms, no uncertainty – simply get back to Dieppe or further west in one piece and keep on going until you meet up with someone collecting stragglers with a view to reforming as a fighting force.

These were the last orders I received, after that, as you will see, I was on my own so far as being told what to do was concerned.

I personally had no idea what casualties we as a battalion had suffered but now we were certainly no more than a remnant, maybe 10 per cent of our original total with no Commanding Officer, no RSM and not many men from the rifle companies. It was strange really to be so broken up – surely all this destruction could not have been caused by one air raid, could it?

Severe and prolonged as it had been during my experience of it last night, the effects seemed to be incredible and I began to wonder, in all seriousness, who would be paying for all this. All the equipment we had lost, all that had been burnt and abandoned. The position we were now in was that to go forward or to stay where we were was to meet captivity or death, the only sensible thing therefore was to go back, on the principle that 'he who lives, lives to fight another day'.

The CSM told us about the route to take – he said, 'Keep going west with the sun either on your left if it's near midday or in your eyes if it's evening, cross the river by the bridge we've used if you can reach it, swim the water otherwise, and keep on going, keep on going come hell or high water.'

'Good luck, lads,' he finished with. 'See you later.'

Before we broke up and moved off someone rather anxiously asked about food and the Sergeant Major said, 'Oh aye, right lads, it's hardly worth telling you about, there's so little of it I nearly forgot to tell you; hold yer forage caps out and we'll share out what bit of food we've got.'

So, I, like everyone near me whom I could see, got a cap full of 'Sun Pat' raisins, pulled out of a sack by a corporal and shared out by his big dirty hand, and a large oval tin of pilchards in tomato sauce. Where these came from I didn't know and I thought it was unwise to ask – you don't query where food comes from in such circumstances. I suppose they could have come from the Abbeville area from an abandoned corner shop when the Adjutant sent back for instructions.

And of course I still had my unopened tin of iron rations which I was dying to open to see what was inside. Later I found it was rich, hard, plain chocolate, like solid cocoa. Thus I set off on this journey of a lifetime somewhat inadequately provisioned!

We moved off in small parties at a few minute intervals, and I must say I felt very emotional at this point. As I've said before, we had come down from a battalion of over 600 men, fully equipped, part of a brigade and part of a division, and now I was down to a small ragged party of five or six mates; it was like the nursery rhyme of ten little nigger boys but on a much bigger scale!

I had set off on a troop train and met up with other trains with trucks, Bren carriers, ammunition and guns followed up behind with more infantry battalions, but now it was all gone and I still hadn't even seen a German yet, much less killed one. I was almost alone, on foot with not much food – and it was a good job I was pretty fit as otherwise I would have been a dead duck in no time.

I was armed with a Bren gun from somewhere, probably from one of the trains during the bombing the day before, with plenty of ammunition and I had a pocket full of raisins, some pilchards and a tin of hard chocolate, and that was it – all I was likely to get for some time to come. But it was very frustrating.

We set off when it was our turn and we were soon among the refugees again, more military this time and as we got nearer the river or canal, which was some miles miles away from where we rejoined the crowd, the noise of artillery got louder than ever over towards Abbeville. There was also a faint never-ending sound of machine-gun fire giving every sign that a battle north of Abbeville was growing more vicious with close fighting as the day wore on towards nightfall. The noise slowly got worse as we neared the area where we knew the bridge was, more insistent, more defined and I began to wonder if we were going to make it and succeed in crossing the water. The fighting was definitely getting closer, and I for one didn't like the sound of it.

Then an amazing thing happened as we got nearer the bridge, which we had learned was called Pont Laviers – the crowd of refugees suddenly seemed to disappear as we sat down for a short rest, and before we could make out the significance of this, two or three German motorcycle-sidecar units fitted with machine-guns on the sidecars suddenly came into view, round a bend in this left-hand curving road about seventy feet away like a deadly apparition and there they were, almost on top of us like emissaries of Satan or the Grim Reaper. We, the five or six of us, were at that moment sat down on a low wall at the side of the road having a breather after walking ten miles or so with our weapons, including the two or three Brens in our possession, across our knees pointing to the left towards where the Germans came from. Without thinking about it we with the Brens opened fire and shot all the motor cyclists in a matter of seconds with long bursts. The bikes crashed and, because motorcycle troops like these cannot really take prisoners, what would have been a nasty moment for us, was over before it had even started.

The speed of our reaction surprised me – I know we had loaded Bren guns across our knees, ready to fire, and pointing in the direction of the Germans but really they were hit by several bursts of gunfire probably before they even recognised us. No doubt we were tensed up by the noise of battle not too far away and so were more ready to fire mentally. We moved on quickly after this, the last thing we wanted was to be caught on this road by the follow-up parties of German infantry coming on behind who would not be too chuffed when they came across their dead mates.

When we eventually reached the bridge it was nearly dusk and it was quiet and peaceful again, a kind of warm summer's evening and the refugees seemed to have eased off temporarily. Nearby was a sort of a quay, perhaps where boats pulled in off the canal to load or unload, and parked on it was a magnificent six-wheeled troop transporter, a Berliez of the French Army with four rows of seats in the

Typical German forces in France, 1940
(Pictures courtesy of Bundesarchiv, Koblenz)

canvas-covered back. It seemed wicked to leave it there for the Germans, because it could not be driven across the canal, so we decided to drive it into the water, over the edge of the quay. We got the engine running easily enough, but the brakes were hard on, and we couldn't get them off no matter what we did. And of course we could not waste too much time here on the wrong side of the water. Finally we assumed that someone must have cut the vacuum brake pipes and therefore until these were repaired no one was going to move this 10-ton truck. So we had to leave it and get across the canal while there was still a glimmer of light to see our way across the by now damaged structure.

Once across the canal or river I lost my mates as there seemed to be an enormous crush of refugees again, now mainly military, coming up the tow path on the western side from the direction of Abbeville. There were men from all the armies ever engaged against the Germans in this war – Poles, French, Czechs, Belgian, Dutch, British – some wounded with bloody bandages on their heads, their limbs, their bodies. Hundreds of men, thousands in fact. I was fascinated by the mixture of hats, helmets, uniforms, weapons, languages. This was the detritus, the debris, of war and there must have been some desperately serious battles nearby to the north and east of Abbeville or Amiens to cause all this.

Men of the Royal Engineers in this stream, with whom I was able to have a word to get their news, told me they had been engaged in street fighting in the centre of Amiens from the sewers, rolling bundles of sticks of dynamite under the tanks as they clattered down the streets below which the Engineers were hiding in a kind of subterranean ambush. They destroyed a number of tanks but lost a lot of their men when German infantry penetrated the sewers seeking them out. All this talk, unwise curiosity on my part, and watching the endless streams of soldiers and civvies kept me in the area, wandering down towards Abbeville centre away from the remnants of the bridge.

I began to think I would be better off nearer the centre as I would probably find a main road to Dieppe, or might even find some transport, maybe a train. You never know your luck! The crowd here was really like that of a football match but by now it was getting dark, a very deep grey-blue dusk, though not black dark yet, probably near 7 p.m. Oddly enough, among all these people, I felt quite safe in this bizarre scene. Stupidly, I felt nothing was likely to harm us as we were now on the western side, i.e. the safe side of the water. And as I've already said, it was like being in a football crowd going home after the match was over.

Then, unexpectedly there was a low roar of engines, getting louder and louder very quickly and I saw several streams of twin-engined bombers coming towards us, each stream comprising V-shaped squadrons or flights of seven or nine bombers, there being perhaps eight squadrons or flights per stream, all coming up like the rays of the sun from the south-east quadrant with their apex somewhere overhead, say about 350 bombers in all with probably three tons of bombs on each of them. It was frightening and when I realised what it would all soon mean to us on the ground near the centre of Abbeville without shelter I dived into a dried-up drainage ditch on the west side of the tow path, this seeming to be the most sensible thing to do in the time available.

I landed on top of a girl who was in the ditch before me, who must have wondered what on earth had happened and screamed frantically until I wriggled off her without poking any part of my body above the ditch. Fortunately the ditch was quite dry, full of grass and wild flowers, and then within seconds the terrible bombing of Abbeville began. Perhaps this was a retaliation for the fighting and resistance we had heard earlier, or else to ensure that a salient could not be created on the left flank of the Panzer Army we had seen moving towards the Channel ports.

The bombs came with a rush, in sticks of six generally, which

Abbeville centre after the bombing of 1940 (Photograph courtesy of Madame Legrand)

More views of Abbeville centre after the bombing of 20–21 May 1940
(Photographs courtesy of Madame Legrand)

Abbeville centre

we would count mentally when we knew they were near us, one, two, three, four, jeez that was close, five that's near, six. And so it went on for about thirty minutes, interspersed with great clusters of incendiary bombs, maybe 3,000 in each plane, and the enormous explosions of landmines every so often. These seemed to make the very ground ripple where I was lying in the ditch at the side of this sobbing girl. The big bombs of perhaps 1,000 kilos penetrated deep into the foundations of buildings and streets, with their interlaced water pipes, gas mains, electricity cables and so on, before they exploded with cataclysmic effect. The sky over the centre of Abbeville quickly became a lurid glow as the fires took hold, punctuated by the flashes of the rippling heavy explosions. Calculating back from the numbers of aircraft involved, say about 350 to 400, there must have been 150,000 incendiary bombs with 100 landmines, 200 of the 1,000-kilo bombs and about 5,000 smaller bombs. And there was no opposition either, no fighter aircraft, very little AA fire, just we refugees and the civvies of Abbeville.

It was all over in about thirty minutes, leaving the whole of the centre of the city covered in a huge red glow reflecting from the smoke cloud canopy.

As the last planes were turning away it went relatively quiet and I got to my feet, very shaken as I gave my hand to the unknown girl and helped her up. I think I was shell shocked to some extent by it all or suffering from amnesia as I have no recollection of how, some twenty-four hours later, I was clear of Abbeville, and on a main road heading in a westerly direction, hopefully making for Dieppe as the Sergeant Major had said. There had been a lot of activity in the last twenty-four hours – shooting, observing, bombing, refugees both civil or military – but I had no real recollection of it all then and certainly could not give an account of myself if asked.

Yet, somewhat surprisingly, I was still alive, despite all that had happened since the bombing of our trains in the railway yard the day before.

Today was Wednesday, 22 May, though the day before, 21 May, was a blank to me at the time. Again it was getting dark; it was so confusing.

After that I simply went where the crowd went, away from Abbeville but not knowing where we were going. I must have felt safe within them, like a tiny fish in the midst of a gigantic shoal when predators circle around. That's all there was to it for me, no maps, no plan, no fresh orders – just keep going and try to obey the last order if that were possible.

Chapter III

Abbeville to Dieppe on Foot

It was now late on 22 May, it was dark and I was tramping away from the fires of Abbeville in the direction of Dieppe, or so I hoped. I cannot remember any of the events of this day, how and why I got away from Abbeville, what direction I took, who was with me, where we ate and drank, it was all a blank. Nor can I remember too much of the previous day either. All I do know is that there were no KOYLIs with me and somehow I was on the road towards Eu with an automatic weapon, the Bren, which I liked, with two full magazines in my weapon pouches and a few loose cartridges and clips of five in my pockets.

I do not think I was too far out of Abbeville, maybe 10 km towards the north-west. I was in an endless stream of refugees, both civil and military with the usual cars, carts and people on foot with their suitcases. We plodded along, by now without much hope of getting anywhere useful before, as we saw it, we were overrun by the leading elements of enemy armoured formations which we expected would soon be moving into areas to the west of the Somme. It was a grisly expectation for all of us, civil and military, and if it happened we would have to surrender and be taken prisoner.

Then, unexpectedly, late at night, we were stopped at a military road block, a combined French and British block which directed military stragglers, the good, the bad and the indifferent, to where they could do most good and be most useful in this little area. I, after being questioned at length about my training and showing them my army pay book, my AB64 (which I still have), was sent off up a lane towards the north where after about half a mile an officer put me on a Vickers machine-gun, unmanned but already partially set up. I must have told them I knew how to use machine-guns during my interrogation but I can't remember this now. Some time later another soldier was sent up to help me.

We set the gun up properly on its tripod, mounted it conveniently at the side of and to the rear of a substantial tree whose trunk, of about thirty-inch diameter, would give us some protection if needed. I fed the end of a belt of ammunition into the breech, arranged the rest of the belt neatly in the ammo box, showed my mate how to keep the belt feeding nicely if I began firing in earnest, got the water circulation system piped up, fired off perhaps twenty-five rounds to check the feed, the ammo, and cooling system and then sat down to await events. All this, of course, was carried out in semi-darkness, aided by striking a match when necessary, but avoiding creating too much light for too long for fear of snipers.

A little while later a sergeant came along to see us, and being assured the set-up was now OK and ready for action, told us he would send up some food. My oh my, and was I hungry by now! This was something, my first real hot meal in a proper mess tin with a knife and fork since leaving Rennes nearly a week before, so there must have been a proper cookhouse or else a civilian French café nearby, though it was out of sight. And this wasn't all we got, as the Sergeant later gave me a ration, which was a full gill, of neat Navy rum, the second time I had been given such rum by the Army in France.

Believe me it was beautiful stuff; we called it 'mother's milk' in all sincerity because you could drink this high-strength, sweet alcohol neat, straight off like warm cocoa. And when it got down in your stomach, without burning your throat like whisky does, it would burst out generating a feeling of warmth and well-being, driving out all cold, hunger, anxiety and fear. This is very different from the rums I have drunk in civilian life away from the Army. Another surprise to me was that the full gill of this rum, taken as we did undiluted, did not make me drunk or stupid; I just felt relaxed, confident and sure of myself. This was what we needed on that cool night, on a ridge, waiting for whatever dangers the enemy would bring before long.

Politicians, in Parliament, were later to stop the supply of this rum and I for one who had drunk it in the right circumstances would never forgive them, or the people who put them up to it, for stopping our rum ration.

When early morning came and with it the daylight, we could see we were on the forward slope of a ridge running nearly due north with the machine-gun set up on the eastern side of a sunken lane. The lane ran parallel with the ridge, and about 100 yards down from it, with a line of big trees and masses of gorse, shrubbery, bushes and brambles along the sides of the lane and behind us to the top of the ridge. The ground immediately in front of us, facing the east, included a thin hedge and a broken wall with wire strung along its length and a rough fence near us before it opened out into more grassy fields with occasional trees in them. These fields ran down to a river or big stream in a valley maybe half a mile away and open fields and isolated hedgerows occupied the ground between us and the stream. To our left, a hedge with some intermittent solid stone walls ran up at an angle across our front to join our lane far over on the right, in the direction of the main road. This hedge seemed to emerge from a wooded area down in the valley near the river to our left. Roughly in front of me, about 300 yards away, was a gap in a wall portion of the hedge which looked to be for the purpose of letting animals through from one field to another, though there were no animals in these fields now. It was typical Norman farmland.

All in all, it looked to be ideal for an infantry attack from the east where the enemy was known to be. Well over on our left, on something of a plateau maybe half a mile away up the lane, there was a battery of what looked like 3.7 AA guns, about 90mm calibre. They might have been French guns, not British, and some of them looked as if they were fitted with a magazine feed mechanism holding four or five shells. They certainly had a great lump of a thing above the breach block which could have been a magazine. We had heard about these dual-purpose guns though we had never seen one so it was quite reassuring to know we had some to back us up in case we were attacked by dive-bombers. This looked to be something of a real defence position now as during the night many more troops had come in to reinforce us; indeed there were now more French troops here than British, though of course I could only see my own little patch – what lay out of sight I had no means of knowing.

Activity became apparent when a few Germans in green uniforms dashed up behind the hedge and across the gap to my front, obviously trying to make their way to the right end of our lane, i.e. towards the main road. Then mortar bombs started bursting along the front side of the ridge, near the line of our position, as the German mortar crews opened fire to support their infantry. They were not on target, though, so we were unaffected really and their support was not very strong. Then we saw more vague shapes in the woods below, crossing the stream and coming along several hedges towards us. It was an attack in company strength at least and without waiting any longer for orders I joined in the general firing which was breaking out along the ridge, aiming on the hedge to my front, traversing my fire to left and right over a narrow arc. It did not seem to have much effect, however, and I decided to concentrate on the gap in the wall where Germans kept dashing across in small parties. They were very quick however and I didn't really catch any of them. I began to worry that more and more Germans would be able to get round behind us from the right and that could become dangerous if they attacked up the lane in an effort to dislodge us.

So, finally, I decided to direct my aim at the right-hand end of the gap and then when I saw movement at the other end, through the corner of my eye, let rip in long bursts so that with luck some of the Germans were bound to run into the stream of bullets, pouring out at a rate of about ten rounds per second. It was an effective tactic, I kept catching some and fairly quickly they stopped coming. Mortar bombs still kept bursting along the ridge and the lane as the Germans retreated from the positions on the right but none of the bombs burst near me and so my firing was unaffected. Further fire from light automatics and the many riflemen stopped this local attack completely and it all went quiet. What was rather disquieting, however, was that during this firing we did not seem to have any support from artillery or mortars. There were no French 75s which I for one was rather hoping for and therefore I felt a heavier German attack would probably be successful and we would be cut off and mopped up.

And all this excitement before we had even had breakfast on that sunny Thursday morning, 23 May.

I should note that at the same time as this desperate little local battle was going on, stories were being told in official French circles that German troops were coming and going on the coast to the north-west of us in the Ault area where motorcycle troops went to the home of one of the local coastal farmers, borrowed his swimming costumes and bought some of his cider! When he asked for payment, as he knew the Germans from his experiences as a POW in the First World War, they said 'tomorrow'; they came back over a period of several days for a daily swim and a drink, and paid for whatever they had drunk or borrowed. And this was while we were fighting them only twenty miles away.

Talking later with my mate on the Vickers, he said we had been damn lucky, a mortar bomb, 50 mm, I should think, was stuck in the roots on the left of the tree behind which we were sheltering –

without exploding! Had it burst a few feet to the east or west of this tree we would probably have been goners. He said the bomb was hot, a dull-red colour. And I didn't even know it had landed because of the noise and steam from the gun I was firing. Somehow one is taken over by the excitement of it all in these circumstances and nothing counts any more, near misses are misses and one goes on regardless of events.

We got a bit of breakfast – rolls of US bacon in bread and butter, tea and more rum, so up to a point we were well catered for while it was all peaceful again. More ammunition was brought up, the machine-gun was cleaned, I topped up the cooling system from a petrol can filled with water and soon we were ready for another go if the enemy came again.

A few hours later, after the abortive infantry attack, we were in real trouble when Stukas came over, maybe ten of them, to dive-bomb us with their 500-kilo impact-detonation screaming bombs. They were a terrifying weapon against civilians and poorly organised troops when there were no or few air defences but we had a battery to defend us – though it was only a temporary defence really because as soon as the Stukas became aware of the guns they directed their attack against them instead of us and quickly silenced all of them except one or two for the loss of a few Stukas which crashed headlong into the ground in massive fireballs. There was then a pause and we were able to get another snack of sorts from Royal Navy biscuits and corned beef. Lunch perhaps, but then they came back in full strength, the enemy infantry with more Stukas and a few tanks supporting them. We could see the ground forces about 1,000 yards away, vaguely among the trees as before, when it all started again but much more seriously and determined this time.

Three or four tanks with the infantry behind them came up the left-hand side as the Stukas attacked that side and the last of the guns. One gun was quickly knocked out but as the Stukas turned away and flew off preparatory to making another dive-bombing attack, one of the last guns, which was magazine-fed, was lowered right down to fire down the slope at the advancing tanks over almost open sights. In a matter of minutes the leading tanks were hit by heavy shells, 90mm or slightly bigger, explosive AA shells rather than armour-piercing ones, though I expect they had the same equally high muzzle velocity. This gun became an equivalent, for the time being, of the famous German 88mm anti-tank gun we were to hear so much of later in the War. I never heard of British or French AA guns being used in this same way again and I've often wondered why. The tanks became fireballs from their exploding ammunition and fuel and, like the Stukas, which had flown away by now, no more tanks joined the battle so the enemy infantry pulled back too.

The attack seemed to fizzle out after this and we had some hours peace and quiet up to nightfall, though we felt sure the respite would not last indefinitely. To our surprise, however, tomorrow was to be another day for someone else, because when it got dark a British officer, a major, came up the lane from the road on the right calling out for British soldiers to hand over their positions and heavy weapons to the French, who would be taking over from us, and ordering us to make our way down the lane back to the main road and then on to Dieppe, where a new British defence force was to be formed.

So before midnight I was on my way again walking back towards the west only this time with more British troops to accompany me. Much happier now as a result of all this action and because I was no longer alone, I set off walking with a lighter step than hitherto. It was now nearing midnight on what I thought must still be 23 May. It had been a very busy and active day, we had had our brief moments of glory perhaps and though I badly wanted a sleep, there was no time to waste here. We knew the Germans were nearby to the east and could break through this line which we had just been ordered to leave when the French took over from us. So, like Felix, the famous cartoon cat, I kept on walking throughout the night, resting occasionally and then going on again. After a few hours on the road we were stopped once more by French officers who wanted to know our start point and our ultimate destination before letting us continue to the west.

At dawn on the next day, 24 May, we got up from the roadside where we had been napping and joined the refugee stream of 'Les Miserables' once again. It became a warm day, as every day seemed to be these days, with a hot sun and we were thankful for the fine weather – at least we had not suffered any rain which would have been a killer for all concerned. We were also grateful for the lines of trees, plane and poplar, which we were told had been planted by Napoleon Bonaparte for his troops 150 years before to keep them shaded from just such a sun as this. During this feeling of satisfaction with life in general, we suddenly heard again the roar of aero engines approaching and several Messerschmitt 109s at low tree-top height, flew down the road from the east, machine-gunning as they came, swept up and round to turn through 360 degrees and then repeated the attack. What amazed me in this, which was repeated several times, was the speed at which the beaten zone of the bullets in the road swept up towards me. I would be perhaps a quarter of a mile away from the first strikes, perfectly safe you might think, and in seconds the strikes were all over the road surface in front of me while I cowered behind one of the trunks of the trees at the side of the road.

My God, it was fast! In what seemed to be a few seconds bullets would be streaming up the road and bits of branches, leaves, twigs etc. would be slowly falling like snowflakes. A group of we soldiers, from a mixture of regiments and corps, each behind a tree on the roadside, began firing towards the approaching aircraft on command from an unofficial sentry and so created a zone of fire from the several Brens and twenty rifles or so, which the

Messerschmitts must fly through. Whether it was this fire, or they simply got fed up, I don't know but they cleared off though without any being hit, so far as I could see. We resumed our march, or walk, and continued on our way towards Dieppe; we were lucky because I don't think any of our men were hit in this attack, though some of the civvies who were with us caught it and one or two of the horses. Seeing wounded and dying horses kicking and threshing about with blood in evidence is quite sickening, because you can't do anything for them except put a shot through the head.

Some short while after this the stream of people and carts came to a standstill. We went forward to investigate what was causing the hold-up and found it was an almighty traffic jam on a long downhill stretch of road curving to the right down through a hollow and up the next hill. There was a kind of escarpment on the right of the road where the gradient of the ground was more severe than that of the road. Cars had been abandoned here, and in the hollow, because I think they had been freewheeling as far as they could when they had run out of petrol.

Now, because the road was blocked by them, wheeled traffic of all types was piling up, unable to get past and so creating a real gridlock with car horns being impatiently sounded, horses neighing, donkeys braying and everyone becoming excited. An officer stuck in a staff car saw us coming up through the crowd of walkers and told us to clear the road. Just like that – as Tommy Cooper might have said.

'Clear the road' he said.

We looked at one another, rather stunned by the order, and someone with us said, 'How are we to do that, sir?'

'There's about thirty of you, big, young, strong lads, so start pushing those cars down the ravine and don't mess about,' he said,

An NCO, perhaps a corporal, told a group of us to start pushing vehicles over the side of the road down into the ravine, so as to make some room by which the gridlock could be broken. And broken it was, at a cost of about seven abandoned cars and a truck. Before the staff car moved off, though not moving much faster than us, the officer, a major I think, said, 'Well done, lads, a good job, there will be a lot of folk grateful to you, good luck.'

I think he was a bit sorry for us, having seen the expression of distaste on our faces, when at his command we did for these perfectly good cars.

The refugee procession of people, carts, vans, cars, and the staff car, moved off and we got on our way without any more incidents delaying us.

Sometime after this we had what turned out to be a real stroke of luck. A main railway line with two or three tracks came alongside the road and we could see there were several trains on it, a train traffic jam! Some were the same type of wooden troop trains we had travelled in nearly a week before and one was a posh civilian train. As we got nearer the troop trains, men appeared in the doorways of one of them and began to shout to us – incredibly they were Duke of Wellingtons among others. I was amazed to see them, so I went down to talk and then I joined them on the train along with a few of my new mates from the day before in the hopes of hearing from them some news of the missing KOYLIs.

The 'Dirty Dukes', as we called them, told me they had been in this train nearly two days, moving a bit and stopping a lot and that they were living in hopes of reaching Dieppe sometime. I told them of the later raids on Abbeville, of which they seemed to know nothing, and the attack on us the previous day. I said that if the trains didn't get moving very soon we had better all start walking towards the west like we were doing before we met the trains. If we didn't resume our trek fairly quickly I reckoned we'd soon be walking back east on our way to a German prison camp. However, before there was time for a decision on this key issue of whether it was better to set off walking or stay on the train, the trains started moving forward at a good walking pace. So I quickly jumped on board and cheered up in consequence. I felt I'd done enough walking for a bit and the thought of a train ride to Dieppe was most attractive. Indeed I might even be there before nightfall and be tucking into a good meal in some transit camp.

There were two troop trains now, moving side by side; men in the other train opened their sliding doors and I saw some were Green Howards, and there were also Yorks and Lancs – a real mixed bag of northern infantry regiments. Some began jumping from one train to the other, what became an exciting game trying to find the faster train as one train pulled in front of the other. I saw quite a few slip as they jumped and though we held our hands to them, shouting to them to grab us, they missed our outstretched hands and fell on the track. I don't know what happened to them after that as they were left behind. I just hoped they were not crushed by the wheels.

Soon, however, the train I was on moved away from the other and left it well behind. We eventually came up alongside the civilian train we had seen originally and we ran side by side for some time. We could see the civvies packed into it, standing in the corridors and so on, really packed, almost like sardines – all very smart however, compared to our old trucks; there was even a big restaurant car. As we overtook this train, I saw it was a long one, maybe fourteen coaches with luggage cars at the rear and everywhere packed with people. We then slowed down as the civvy train overtook us and moved away much faster and out of sight.

Our train stopped again, however, and after a bit I began to mentally calculate how long I should wait before I ought to leave the train and move on to the west on foot; we had gained maybe five miles since I had been on the train so I could afford to wait perhaps half an hour but I didn't want to waste too much time. We had not been waiting long, however, when we saw and heard groups of bombers going in the direction of Dieppe and shortly after the sound and vibration of heavy bombs bursting on or near the track, our track.

We decided that if they had hit the track, probably seven to ten miles further on, it would be the end of this rail service to Dieppe. This temporary service probably began somewhere over to the east, as near Abbeville as they could reach now that I knew the Germans had crossed the Somme. I reasoned I had better be ready to start walking again fairly soon if the train I was on was not going to go anywhere. But, reluctant to leave the train, I decided to wait a bit longer to see what would happen – after all we were not sure the track was cut by the bombing we had just heard. I'd noticed before that the French railway staff I had met had been hard working and patriotic. They did their duty right up to the limit, so I had some confidence in them. Our train waited for a time and I waited with it, somewhat impatiently. Then in the early evening we set off again at a walking pace. Perhaps an hour later we stopped and this time the engine driver and his fireman walked down the side of the train saying, '*C'est fini.*'

It was a case of all change, a full stop, the terminus! The stop was because the civvy train, which was now just ahead of us, maybe half a mile away, had been bombed, with the track on which both trains were standing being cut.

I left our train, walked forward and saw that the civvy train was a mess with the engine partly in a crater; the front carriages were derailed and leaning over and the rear carriages and luggage vans, while still on the track, had been badly shot up. All the track up near the engine was a series of craters, with part of the embankment gone too.

I climbed aboard the rear of the train and worked my way through it, slowly, and with some trepidation, looking in all the compartments. Many were empty, but there were quite a few dead people in there, corpses. Most of them were lying back in the seats, propped up against the back of the upholstery where they had died after being hit by fighter aircraft which I assumed had shot up the coaches following the bombing. A few bodies had fallen forward and lay on the floor; maybe they had been shot in the chest or in the stomach rather than in the top of their heads like the other corpses which appeared to be sitting back in their seats. It was a dreadful bloody scene, the like of which I had never encountered before. Some particularly harrowing sights were in the first-class coaches where immaculately dressed young women, wearing expensive pearl necklaces, beautiful jewellery and fur coats, would be flopped over with a little dried blood staining the floor of the coach, the seats and their clothing. Death, seen at such close quarters, really brings out the horror of war in a way that no politician's talk can.

Fortunately only a small number of corpses were there, compared to the number of people on the train as we saw it earlier, so presumably all the wounded had been got away by the survivors. The people I saw were mostly well dressed and well to do with their expensive possessions. Whether there had been any ordinary lower-class people on this train cannot be surmised. Someone told me later that this train had originally started its journey in Amsterdam or Brussels so maybe it had been a way of escape only for those who could afford it. The other ordinary mortals either stayed where they were, walked, or took a cart. Well down the train I came across the dining car, badly damaged with broken bottles everywhere and the barman dead in the exit from the car. There was little food left apart from a few sandwiches on a china plate. I took some and salvaged two bottles of champagne out of a cabinet and left that wreck of a train.

I walked on along the track in what I thought would be in the general direction of Dieppe and within an hour or so, still in semi daylight, I came on a small party of British soldiers, presumably a guard. They again checked my pay book and after asking a few questions, directed me round a rather unobtrusive bend leading off into a kind of semi-camouflaged siding. This turn off the main railway lines led through some trees into the biggest depot of Nissen huts and other buildings that I had ever seen or even heard of.

I later found out when I investigated that this depot was stocked with food, stores, ammunition, light weapons and mountains of fuel in 40-gallon drums. It included a hospital and dining rooms, barracks, armoury – you name it, it was there! It was the depot at Eu, maybe a third of the way from Dieppe to Abbeville and 2 or 3 km from the sea. To me at that moment it was an Aladdin's cave filled with everything I needed!

Then of all things, while I was looking across at the several sets of railway lines which formed a big siding or marshalling yard in front of a row of the bigger buildings, end on to the lines into which they led, who should I see at that very moment, driving a small loco up and down a length of straight track at the front of these sidings, but Lieutenant Lee, our Intelligence Officer, and my boss.

He was about 100 feet away from me and the loco was going towards the entrance to the siding and the way out to the main line. Before I was able to shout to him to stop, however, he was gone under the trees and away, so I couldn't report to him and ask, perhaps mischievously, whether there were any further orders. He was one of the officers who told us, when we broke up at the other side of Abbeville, to make for Dieppe and the Channel coast. He disappeared, however, before I could reach him and I never saw him again. With hindsight I suppose he used the loco to make his way to Dieppe and with any luck he'd be there before nightfall.

Somewhat saddened by this unexpected turn of events, I made my way finally into the depot. There were a few soldiers about and NCOs but not many and I saw no officers, which was rather a surprise. Having seen the guard at the entrance I was expecting to find myself in a properly functioning unit of the RASC, so I was disappointed.

A stew with potatoes was on the go – soldiers on active service always seem to be able to make some food given half a chance – so I took a mess tin full, and a mug of tea. I then found a bed in the hospital, got some clean blankets and went off to sleep as soon as I had eaten, thankful to be in a proper bed for the first time in months.

The next day, after a really good night's sleep and a breakfast of sorts, with cold American bacon, bread and endless mugs of tea, I set off to really explore the depot. I shouldn't call it a depot really as no one in authority seemed to be organising anything; it just was an abandoned army central stores, and a very big one at that, but certain things were working, such as the supply of hot water, so we had showers available in a medical block. There was also a canteen and cookhouse operating. The big stores warehouses, however, were all open for men to help themselves, though some RAOC people were still in the armouries.

I helped myself to a new uniform, except for the battledress blouse, as I didn't want to have to transfer my regimental badges and divisional signs from the old blouse to the new, with a new set of underwear, socks and shirt though I kept my old boots as they were well worn in. Then I had a shower, a shave and felt a new man. A word with a senior armourer I met in the armoury of this depot or dump and I got myself two extra Bren magazines, two new barrels for the Bren and three bandoleers of .303 ammunition. Each bandoleer contained fifty rounds, one bandoleer being tracer and the others standard rounds. Then back to my bed to fill the two new magazines with sixty of my extra rounds of ammo, half being tracer, and as soon as I had cleaned the Bren I was ready for business again.

While walking round the depot again after this I saw a new lot of maybe twenty or thirty stragglers limping and staggering down a gravelly track or lane connecting the depot to the main road running past it on higher ground behind the trees. I went up the track to help them carry some of their rifles and to my absolute astonishment there was my old friend from way back, Geoffrey Grimshaw in this lot looking absolutely shattered. It was the first time I'd seen him since before we left Rennes over a week before. It was incredible for us to meet like this, by chance in the middle of this war zone, me rejuvenated after maybe eighteen hours there and he a limping wreck.

My first words to him were: 'God Geoff, where have you been, what's happened?'

'Get me somewhere where I can sleep, I'm all washed up,' he said.

I helped him into the hospital block where I was to a bed next to mine, took his boots and blouse off, got him some tea and then let him sleep untill the next day, maybe for twenty-four hours.

I then went playing Robinson Crusoe again to get a fresh set of kit for Geoff ready for the next day when I expected he would have a shower, shave and so on. I think I cleaned his rifle for him, polished his boots and generally tidied up his kit. When I was doing these various small jobs for my comrade, I found he had no ammunition for his rifle.

Why was this? I wondered, though I never asked him – a Light Infantryman who could not defend himself because he had no ammunition.

I also went in the medical stores and found a first-aid manual, a small leather-bound book which I thought would be useful; even more useful I found a steel tin, about the size of an iron ration, which contained a glass and steel hypodermic and ten glass capsules of morphia with instructions how to use them, and the dosage. This I reckoned would come in very handy if the worst came to the worst at some time in the near future and I or one of my companions was in severe pain from serious wounds. And if I ever did get out of this mess and back to England without needing to use morphia, I could always hand it in at the first QM stores I came across. So it wouldn't be lost.

Next day, after a good night's sleep, a big breakfast of bacon again for the pair of us, with tinned tomatoes this time, bread and tea, a shower and shave for Geoff, we were ready for the off, he fairly refreshed in his nice new uniform after the overnight rest of nearly twenty-four hours.

Here I must digress slightly, as with my two nearly filled bandoleers round my shoulders, carrying the Bren in my right hand with its spare barrel on top of my pack, and my two full magazines in my breast pouches, Geoff said I looked like Pancho Villa, the famous Mexican guerrilla leader of 1912. That name always stuck to me, and from then on I was always Pancho to Geoff.

I gave him one of the two bottles of champagne I had salvaged from the train, which he stuffed down his blouse and we set off walking, hopefully for Dieppe, in mid-morning on that sunny day. We walked via the stony track leading up the hill out of the depot to join the main road, the reverse route to that taken by Geoff on his arrival the previous day. Oddly enough no one else accompanied us, almost as if they didn't want to leave the comfort of the depot. Perhaps they thought subconsciously that in due course, in a few days, they would be rescued by an advancing Anglo/French army.

The road was full as usual with streams of refugees and stragglers now it was daylight and mid-morning. They seemed to rest up somehow somewhere during the night but got on the road again at daybreak. We hadn't been walking more than half an hour with them when I heard a loud crash of breaking glass and Geoff shouting out that he had dropped the champagne and broken it. Of all things to happen now, and champagne bottles don't usually break as easy as that. I could have kicked him – catastrophe! Now he had no refreshment of his own and so he'd just have to stick with me, whether he liked it or not in order to share mine.

We kept on going steadily forward, but with frequent rests, as Geoff wasn't too fit; to be blunt about it he'd had a relatively easier life than I up to the time of the move away from Rennes. First he was a truck driver, even in England, fetching rations, and later a motorcycle despatch rider making trips between battalion and brigade or division while I had been a foot slogger ever since the New Year. I had gradually become physically fit, even to the extent of having to do thirty minutes physical training every morning, after I had moved away from my clerical job in the QM stores. I had to accept the rather hard daily training and so I was better able to cope with the extreme efforts now being called for.

By about noon there was a sudden flurry of activity when a group of Stukas and Messerschmitts attacked and dive-bombed a crossroads village just ahead of us, maybe half a mile away. The bombing was intense followed up by low-level machine-gunning – we were so near we could feel the ground vibrations of the bombs and we really feared we could be caught up in it. But it was all over in seconds; there was no time to even think of opening fire. The village was a hub or meeting point of at least five roads and was clearly a good military target, ignoring the civilians, and I should think it was hit by at least twenty big, screaming Stuka bombs in a matter of seconds. We got to the village perhaps a quarter of an hour later, after most of the mercifully few casualties were being attended to as it would seem that most of the refugee civilians had scattered immediately they heard the arcraft approaching.

I got roped in, however, to help guide a French soldier, who had been blinded by either a bullet or a piece of bomb casing, to a dressing station or surgery which had been set up on the Dieppe side of the village. When I came back to Geoff, who had stayed near the centre of the village where most material damage was concentrated, he was helping to take the corpse of a local woman's husband to an emergency graveyard on the outskirts of the village near a church. It seemed as if this village had been attacked before from the way they were ready with graves for the casualties of an attack.

The body was rolled up in an eiderdown of a floral pattern, red roses I think. Geoff and the widow had an end each of the roll which was curving over and straddling a small, high, two-wheeled cart on which they were taking the corpse to the nearby church. There, from what I could see, a mass grave was being reopened. I relieved the woman of her end and together Geoff and I escorted her and her husband's body, in a solemn procession, to what I suppose would be his last resting place. What rather surprised me in all this was the stoical manner in which these obsequies were conducted, everyone was calm and dignified and there was none of the screaming and hysterics so common today at some burials after acts of violence of this type. We walked away, in silence, impressed by the atmosphere of it all.

We then continued on our way, after watching for a little while as the streams of refugee carts, cars and trucks tried to find an alternative way round the craters in this stricken little village, like ants after an anthill is disturbed. The centre of the village and the strategic crossroads were destroyed so really there was no way through for the vehicles. They seemed to have found another road to the south because we found ourselves alone on the road to Dieppe which was our destination. Perhaps they were heading direct for Rouen with its bridges across the River Seine.

For the first time in our recent experience the stream of refugees had stopped on our road to Dieppe. It was only temporary, we supposed, but it had stopped nevertheless for probably the first time in a week, as a result of the bombing isolating the village from the west. We wondered if this was a new tactic by the Germans to keep the refugees trapped in an area through which the French Army would have to try and bring reinforcements if they were to defend Normandy in the next big offensive.

Still, this was not our problem, so we kept on walking towards Dieppe and as we walked on in the pleasant sunshine Geoff and I swapped experiences. He told me that after leaving Rennes with the road party on the afternoon of 18 May they went up towards Evreaux, near Rouen, and then across the Seine on to somewhere south of Abbeville. On 20 May severe air attacks caused scattering of the convoys and Geoff was diverted into woods well to the south-west of Abbeville. Further air attacks caused a general move south-westwards but Geoff drifted towards the north on his motorbike, got lost and eventually ran out of petrol. Unable to go on with the bike, he then had to abandon it, hidden in a wood. He started walking west after leaving the bike and eventually met up with me at Eu after several days on the road, alone and without much food, water or rest. From my experiences and what I read later it seemed that the Germans were starting to build up a big salient to the west between Abbeville and Amiens from where they would launch their next offensive through Rouen round the back of Paris. Geoff's convoy, unfortunately, got in the way of that salient when it was being planned as the convey moved up towards the Abbeville/Amiens area to cross the Somme. Like us, during our projected crossing of the Somme waterways by train, it was a case of being in the wrong place at the wrong time.

By nightfall we were still many miles from Dieppe and in my heart I began to wonder if we would make it, as I felt tomorrow may well be our last day on the road on foot because of the poor physical state we were now getting into. It was very dark and cloudy, there was no moon or other source of light, and we had reached a section of road which went up a tiring gradient through a cutting with high steep walls on each side of the road, rather like the cutting up Wakefield Road where we lived in Dewsbury.

We had got over halfway up this cutting when we heard the clatter of heavy caterpillar tracks behind us. It sounded very much like a German half-track vehicle or a light tank as it approached the bend at the bottom of the cutting coming up after us.

We had no escape, we could not hide and we could not scale the steep walls which by now must have been twenty feet high like Wakefield cutting, so to me the only thing to do was to shoot out the two masked slit headlights whose beams we could now see sweeping round the corner. It takes much longer to describe than to do.

In seconds I had made my mind up, was down prone on the side of the road in the dry water gully and firing. A quick short burst on one light and the same on the other and they were both out in a matter of a few seconds; the road was in utter darkness again. There was a dead silence, followed by some shouting so Geoff and I took off, running up the sixty or seventy yards to the top of the cutting where we turned off the road and away to safety in the darkness into a field and along behind a hedge. What that vehicle was we never did find out and we did not hear or see it again but it certainly had caterpillars. However, that sudden burst of activity and exertion did us no good at all and we knew we would have to get a lift somehow and very soon.

Some time after this incident it began to rain, heavy soaking rain. We had kept our gas capes as lightweight groundsheets from the earliest days and these kept us fairly dry. This was our first rain in weeks and I knew then from the exhaustion I felt and the misery caused by the rain that a lift was essential, and Geoff was in a worse state than I.

It was now about 4 a.m., early morning, and a few big cars were already on the road heading west, their tyres kicking up spray from the rain as they rushed to get past Dieppe before daylight when they would be exposed to random air attack. God knows where these cars came from but Geoff and I decided to stop one. He said he would do the stopping because he spoke better French than I, and I would stay at the side of the road as back-up. When the next car came into view he stepped forward, like a traffic cop with his arm held up, and expected the car to stop. It did nothing of the sort, almost knocked him down and continued on its journey into the night blowing its horn. We had to wait almost another hour before the next car came and it too behaved in the same manner, nearly killing Geoff in the process. We agreed that we would try again, behaving like gentlemen, and if we got the same reception then we'd behave differently with the fourth car. The third car was the same, it wasn't going to stop for any Allied soldier – we'd have had to be wearing the field grey or green of the Wehrmacht to do any good. So we decided that I, as the marksman, would open fire from the left-hand side of the road with tracer bullets on the driver's side of the car, firing to miss by about two feet, if it did not stop for Geoff when he ordered it to.

It was almost breaking dawn when the next car came, so the driver would have had no excuse if he claimed later that he couldn't see us. Geoff went out for the fourth time, raised his arm, but no sign of a stop so I opened fire, single shots from the Bren. They happened to be tracer bullets and away went three glowing orange balls chasing after the car. It was most dramatic, and I wasn't the one being fired at!

As the car went past, and I had pressed the trigger, I saw it was Belgian. What the devil was it doing down here? I wondered and watched as the orange balls went so slowly past the side of the drivers head, missing him and the car by about two feet. God, did he make an emergency stop! Geoff went up to him and saw that the car was packed with people, all gibbering almost, holding out passports and identity documents.

Geoff told the driver we were an Army road block and needed to know where he was going, why and what a car full of Belgians were doing down here. After some more conversation he told the driver we needed to have a lift to Dieppe, which he offered, so Geoff and I rode on the two running boards, he on the passenger's side and I on the driver's side. At a steady twenty miles an hour, which speed creates a hell of a draft when you are hanging on to a door pillar and riding on the running board, we were in Dieppe in about forty minutes.

After that ride in the wind, I felt so relieved to be still in one piece, it was almost a dubious advantage to have been given a lift; I think I would have almost preferred to have kept on walking.

We left the car, grateful to be in Dieppe and still alive, as it became full daylight, and found ourselves on the outskirts of the town at the top of a hill, presumably leading down to the docks. It was all damp and wet with rain still falling. We now expected to see signs of urgent military activity, troop convoys, tanks, field guns, military police and so on. Instead it was all dead – not a sign of life. Where were the new British formations we expected to find here making ready to move off to do battle with the enemy up the road to Abbeville? There must be units or formations we could join and be back in business again.

After all this effort, we had reached a dead town, not a reborn Aldershot. Oh dear, the disappointment of it for us, plus the thoughts of inevitably more walking – but in which direction?

It was a dilemma and a problem.

Chapter IV

Dieppe to Rouen

It was grey, cold, wet and miserable as we went down the hill into Dieppe town centre and the docks early on the morning of Monday, 27 May, after having had a lift in a Belgian car, commandeered at gun point.

We had hoped to find British forces down there, military police, the Town Major and some of his staff. Even if everyone else had gone, we hoped, indeed we expected, to find signs of the Royal Navy, with some sort of a hot breakfast and a bed perhaps, with none of the hard-tack ships biscuits we had eaten before.

So we went down to the central harbour area of Dieppe, initially cold and wet but optimistic of finding someone who would be of help, past rows of large terraced houses which lined the road on the left-hand western side. On the right-hand side was a sunken river, in a shallow ravine, the Arques I think its name was, which led into the landward end of the harbour. In a way it was like Whitby though Dieppe was rather more sheltered at the harbour's seaward end with the casino and some hotels on a piece of land coming from the west at the sea front to protect the boats and quays in the harbour proper.

In the whole of this two-mile journey down to the quay, and by now it was about breakfast time when we would have expected to see signs of life, we didn't see a soul, no one, not even a cat or a dog. There were no plumes of smoke rising from any of the houses or buildings, indicating that a meal was perhaps being prepared, and not a sound was to be heard. It was a dead town and it became increasingly obvious as we went down the road that everyone had gone, with no troops or police as yet to take their place to ensure security and prevent looting.

When we got down into the harbour, which was normally a hive of civilian activity, with trains running along the quays, the bustle of ships loading and unloading, fishermen active after a night's fishing throwing their boxed catches into the auction sheds for selling, it was all dead. There was no military activity, no stores being unloaded, no marching men, shouting sergeants and corporals; I don't think I even heard much squawking from the gulls. There was a lot of damage to buildings and boats and when we looked carefully we could see many boats were resting on the bottom of the harbour after having been sunk as a result of bombing attacks. Some of the damaged buildings were still smoking slightly, as if the fires created by the last air raid had only just burnt themselves out. To us it looked as if the final raid which had caused much of this devastation had been a big one, probably taking place within the last twenty-four hours, perhaps while we were having our scare with the half-track type vehicle back near Eu or earlier when we witnessed the bombing at the village crossroads.

At the main quay, still tied up to the bollards, but sunk to the bottom of the dock with only the top surface of its deck and its funnels showing clearly through the water, was a big boat. Perhaps it was one of the ferries used up to the outbreak of war on the Newhaven-Dieppe run. These had been converted to hospital ships and one at least appeared to have been sunk as it lay alongside the dock as we could still see the red crosses on it, possibly with helpless casualties on board.

It still seemed to show wisps of smoke from the fires which must have been started before the sinking, though many of the fires on the other wrecked boats in the harbour must have been put out when the boats sank. It seemed odd that wisps of smoke still came up from the hospltal ship – it was almost as if it had only just been attacked whereas I felt it must have been sunk some considerable time earlier. Other smaller boats were partially awash, half sunk shall we say, and they were still smoking. It was all rather odd and most depressing.

Red crosses were visible everywhere on hospital ships, and even through the water we could still see them on this big sunken boat. In all probability, though, they would not have been seen from the air at night by the bomber crews in their Heinkel He111s and their Dornier Do17s. Nevertheless, it was still a sickening sight to see a hospital ship sunk as a result of enemy action.

Peering at the hull through the murky water of the harbour we thought we could just see the ship's name – it seemed to be either King David or St David – though I've never seen any reference to this named boat in the literature. Indeed, after over fifty years, my memory could be wrong and I may be confusing it in my mind with the King David hotel in Jerusalem, which was bombed by Jewish terrorists in 1946 while I was there trying to keep the peace after the War had ended. Recent correspondence with people in Dieppe, to which I shall refer in the bibliography later, leads me to think now, in 1996, that the hospital ship was either the *Maid of Kent* or the *Brighton*, both of which were sunk during the air raids of the 18th and the 21st of May respectively.

I went further along the quay towards the harbour entrance and round towards the hotels and casino in the hope of finding somebody but it was all eerily silent. There was no one, it was very definitely a dead town. Meanwhile, Geoff had gone up alone into what seemed to be the old town of shops, cafes and a market hall but he found nothing and turned back to meet me on the quay as previously arranged. There was nothing to report, we agreed on that, and it was also obvious that there was neither an evacuation nor a reinforcement of the BEF going to take place here, as had been hinted when the remnants of our battalion were ordered to make for the nearest big port along to the west after our disaster at Abbeville. Indeed, Dieppe was the port I was told to make for when I was taken off the Vickers machine-gun after the action against the Germans just west of the Somme river or canal earlier in the week.

We went up a side street together, somewhere near the south or far end of the quay, and there we found our first corpse, that of a young man a bit older than we were, lying by a motorbike just away from the lip of a bomb crater, the crater taking up half the width of the street. The bike was lying on its side and didn't appear to have suffered much damage from the blast. Further up this street we found more corpses but no one living. Who these people were we didn't know; perhaps they were locals who came back to retrieve something from their homes or maybe they were unlucky looters, but whoever they had been they were dead now and would need burying soon. So we retraced our steps and I went right along the quay again towards the far end for a final look around while Geoff went back to examine the bike.

Seeing nothing at this end of town, I came back just in time to hear Geoff starting the bike and after a few hesitant splutters it picked up with a full-bodied roar. It was a 350cc French machine in fairly good nick. Geoff rode it about 100 yards along the quay, came back to me and said, 'He doesn't need it now whereas we do and I don't think I fancy getting to Rouen from here on foot – so what do we do?'

I agreed with him, because I knew he still wasn't in a good enough condition for a long route march and we knew Rouen, which was a hell of a way off, was the obvious place to head for as it gave us the chance to cross the Seine.

So, after thinking it over, I said, 'We'll take the bike, Geoff. You'll be able to drive it, and we'll get it back to Dieppe somehow later. Let's go now without wasting any more time in case another air raid starts.'

So he and I set off for Rouen, 75 km away, feeling just a little bit dubious about taking the bike, though we were agreed on this course of action. As we saw it, in these circumstances of an empty town and more air raids expected at any time, we were only borrowing the bike. Indeed it could be said that we were taking the bike out of a potential war zone to a place of safety. It would, we felt sure, be returned eventually to the owner or his family through the registration details via the number plate. So our consciences were clear as the motor roared into life and we set off up the hill out of the harbour area and away from Dieppe.

At the top of the town there seemed to be a choice of two roads to Rouen, one via the village of Totes about 35 km from Dieppe and the other via Torcy, Pommereval, St Saen's, a big town, Cailly and Isreauville. This was the route we took because without maps at the time it looked to be the more direct one from the way the junction of the two roads was laid out just outside Dieppe. This turned out to be a mistake because it was something of a tortuous route for the first 60 km or so until we joined the main road from Rouen to Neufchatel. This main road went on to Abbeville and Amiens, but we turned right when we joined it, as we wanted Rouen not Abbeville again, or as Eliza Doolittle said 'not bloody lightly'. Then we had easier going for the rest of the journey into Rouen, though we still had the congestion problem caused by refugees, both military and civilian, still coming back from the Amiens area.

However, I am getting ahead of myself in this story as at this moment we had only gone a few kilometres down the road.

Having made our minds up, we got on our way, feeling relieved to have done something positive and decisive regarding ourselves, the bike and the route. We even felt enthusiastic by the way it had all turned out and we could have started singing.

But this feeling of euphoria evaporated after about 40 km or so, say less than an hour's travelling, when we were getting near St

Saen's, I think. We were becoming quite enthusiastic about the thoughts of supper and a real bed in some army reception depot, when suddenly there was an ominous spluttering for a few seconds from the engine, which up to now had been running well, and the bike stopped with a jolt. A deathly silence descended on us and the bike.

After playing around with the engine, Geoff said, 'We've run out of juice, we've had it'.

'What are we gonna do?' said I.

'We're near St Saen's or somewhere big, you can see the town far ahead,' said Geoff. 'It's level road so all we can do is push the bike and hope to get some petrol there, but if we are unlucky we'll abandon the bike and walk on to Rouen even if it kills us.'

So push it we did, it wasn't too bad with two of us at it, and we got to St Saen's or wherever it was after about a couple of hours pushing, cursing and resting. it was a strange thing that I never did find out the name of that place.

We arrived in the town centre, the market square, with all the side streets packed with vehicles such as six-wheeled troop transporters, tanks, jeep-type cars, guns and limbers. The place was packed out. At last, we thought, someone knows there is a war on.

There were all types of white home army French troops with their funny looking 'Art Nouveau' embossed steel helmets plus black French Colonial troops from North Africa and Senegal. We saw Spahis wearing red tarbooshs like Tommy Cooper but with shining black faces, Foreign Legionnaires, and others in blue jackets and floppy white trousers, plus French light infantry dressed in green, with their officers in very smart uniforms with colourful pill-box hats. These men were not wearing flat steel helmets with camouflage netting secured to them and grubby battledress like us, with bandoleers round their necks. It was all extremely colourful and very efficient looking which made us feel a right pair of tramps – we almost felt ashamed to be walking amongst them. But we did wonder what they would be looking like in a week's time.

Geoff told me to hold the bike up at the side of the square while he went to one of the officers sat relaxed in his jeep-type car to beg some petrol, as there were dozens of army trucks and army cars in the vicinity. I suppose he thought they would give him some, five litres, which was only a gallon, without any fuss, from one of their jerrycan-type containers on their vehicles.

But he was way off in assuming this because in no time at all voices were raised and quite an argument was in progress between Geoff and the French officer. I put the bike up on its stand and walked across to join them in an endeavour to calm them down, because Geoff was getting angry and creating increasing tension between himself and this particularly smart-looking young officer. He was sat at his ease in his vehicle, wearing a very smart uniform, beautifully creased, with a bright highly coloured pill-box hat. Geoff, on the other hand, was like a tramp, as I've already said, almost like Charlie Chaplin but not so funny.

I think Geoff had made some derogatory remark about this contrast in dress just before I joined them, which led to the Frenchman drawing his pistol on him as I was walking towards them. At this moment in time I moved quickly up to the left side of the jeep, which was the side of the vehicle nearest to where I had been standing with the bike. The French officer was sat in the driver's seat, which of course was also on this left side. As I approached him I raised my right arm in what I hoped was a sign of peace. He saw me, and suddenly, to my amazement, all the tension unexpectedly evaporated from the situation – after a few quick words to Geoff the French officer drove off to join his column. This was now beginning to move across the square in an easterly direction out of town, and as he went, he gave me a smile. I think I must have looked less of a tramp than Geoff, even though I had the two bandoliers round my neck.

'By God, Geoff,' I said. 'That was a near one.'

'He said I was a scrounger, a deserter,' said Geoff. 'So I was equally blunt about his fancy rig and hat.'

'Anyway,' said I, 'we didn't get any petrol.'

After a short silence while we mulled this over, Geoff said, 'So what are we to do now?'

I reckoned the only thing to do was wait in this town for a few days and try to get some petrol somewhere and if we failed, then we would have to abandon the bike and walk the remaining 50 km or so to Rouen, and hope the fine weather continued. Which is what we said when we ran out of petrol in the first place.

The French troops had moved off by now in the direction of Neufchatel, several hundred of them, motorised, with tanks, guns, limbers, stores lorries and fuel bowsers leaving us alone in the square except for a few odd-looking colonial private soldiers. Looking round us we saw, along a main road leading out of the square towards the west, a large chapel-type of building with a banner along the front saying 'Croix Rouge' with the international symbol of a red cross on a white background. 'Home from home', said I, and we went in to what was a very big hall with a counter along the back manned by a number of local housewives serving home-made coffee, croissants, soup and stew – all very welcoming with a few trestle tables and chairs to make it like a cafe. Through an archway in the side wall was another big room, opening off with its own entrance through big double doors to the street which let light and air into what was clearly a sleeping area.

Geoff went up to the boss lady, told her who we were, adding, and I can hear him now after more than fifty years, '*Nous sommes perdues nos bataillon.*' Not very good French but they knew what he meant and it got us a really good supper, free, and beds for the night, with clean sheets and a blanket, in a far corner of the big bedroom we had just seen. The beds were palliasses filled with straw, army-style which were what we were used to, and Geoff was asleep in no time with the bike standing up on its support stand beside him with the spark plug in his pocket.

I went to the doorway, which was open of course to let fresh air in as probably fifty people of both sexes would be sleeping in this big room. I had a last look round the square and a smoke before turning in; I was in fact running out of cigarettes, having only about two days' supply left and could not cadge any from Geoff because he smoked a pipe.

Then I went back to my corner and sat on the bed, with my back to the wall, thinking for a bit about what we would have to do next if we couldn't get petrol, because this business of petrol worried me. Anyway, we couldn't do anything about it now so I lay on the bed, with the Bren beside me, tied to me with a pull-through, and went to sleep. The Army always said your personal weapon, rifle or light machine-gun, was your best friend and this had been drilled into us for about nine months, so sleeping tied to it was second nature to me.

Near dawn, something roused me from my sleep, an unexpected noise perhaps, and I was wide awake in seconds but without making the slightest movement. One eye opened and I saw, in the light from the doorway, a figure in a tarboosh with a knife glinting in his mouth, or between his teeth, crawling towards Geoff and the upstanding bike situated a few feet away from me. There wasn't a sound in the big dormitory except the breathing and normal turning of some of the sleepers and so it was all the more dramatic in this silent room when as the intruder got nearer after some seconds crawling, I clicked the safety catch off the Bren. My arm was now lying beside the Bren which was kind of semi-cradled in my arm and ready to fire on automatic. The safety catch on this particular Bren, and the associated trigger setting to fire either single shot or automatic, gave out a distinctive metallic noise, sharp and penetrating, which somehow called attention to itself even though it was not noisy in any real sense of the word. Those who heard it knew there was a primed weapon to hand and understood it was not to be trifled with. I saw the crawling man stiffen and he became very still, waiting for some action by me, before I uttered the French command – '*Arretez!*'

Geoff woke immediately and realising what was afoot, got to his feet to get his rifle, but without getting between me and the man, whereupon I got up on my feet. I saw then that he was a French colonial soldier, a black man. I motioned to him to walk towards the doorway, out of the room, on to the street. He was crying and speaking, but I didn't understand what he was saying. As we walked towards the door I wondered what we were going to do with him when we got him out in the street – a bit of a conundrum!

Fortunately for us, a group of French NCOs walked up in the dawn light and with a sense of relief we were able to hand him over to them, Geoff saying '*un voleur*' as we did so. Otherwise, I suppose we'd have had to just let him go, because we couldn't kill him, nor could we take him prisoner. It would be a case of saying '*Allez vous en*', with a few shots fired after him, to chase him off hopefully, but to make sure he got the message and didn't come back with some mates. What would have happened had I not woken at the critical moment I do not know, but later post-wartime experience in 1946 in the Delta area, east of Cairo, showed the common end results of such intrusions were cut throats.

We went back into the sleeping room, a few of the other occupants were awake and Geoff told them briefly what had happened and we all settled down again, though in our case not to sleep. Some time later we were given an early breakfast of coffee and croissants. The staff at the Red Cross told us we could leave the bike with them, in a small locked room for safety, so Geoff and I wandered round this small town to see what there was likely to be of assistance to us. We found a garage near the Croix Rouge but it was locked up and banging on the door didn't elicit any response. Similarly other garages in the town were shut and equally unhelpful.

So we went back to the square and sat down on a seat in the warming sunshine near where we had the fracas the day before with the French officer and waited, like Micawber, for something to turn up. But nothing of interest to us happened – a few French troops moved about, a few army lorries, French, crossed the square on their way to the front we guessed, and a thin stream of refugees came through the town in the direction of Rouen. As the day wore on we began to think we had better resign ourselves to another night in the Red Cross followed by a decent breakfast and then set off early the next day on our long walk of 50 or 60 km to Rouen.

Later in the day, in the early evening near sunset, something did turn up, something very exciting, when a middle-aged Frenchman came up to us and spoke in English! It was incredible to us, that in this little town in the middle of nowhere, at this time, someone spoke near-perfect English. Had we realised it, a lot of the children there must have also spoken English because he was the English teacher from the local lycee, or grammar school.

In answer to his queries we told him briefly of our adventures, where we had been, our names, our regiment, and what we were doing here in his town. He was quite surprised at what we had survived and said he would help us by offering us the hospitality of his home by letting us stay with him and his family until such time as we could get away, either on the bike or walking. We said that it could be a stay of two or three nights, though we couldn't stay any longer as in two or three days' time we would have to start walking if we got no petrol. In any case we should have recovered our physical fitness by then and could no longer justify staying on. So when that was agreed, we collected the bike and went back with our benefactor for a bath, a late evening supper and a good night's rest in a real feather bed. That would be the first time I had slept in a real bed for six months. I had mostly slept on palliasses in the Army and for the last week or so I had been sleeping under hedges except for the two nights in the depot at Eu.

Next day he spoke with someone on the telephone – I think it was someone in authority – because he then came and told us that it was hoped a delivery of petrol, '*l'essence*' to the French, would be arriving very soon in the town and he could almost guarantee we would get enough to take us to Rouen on a motorbike. In the event, after we had been with this family for one whole day and two nights, and becoming increasingly uneasy, we were told that a garage was to receive a small tanker load of '*l'essence*' during the coming night. When I saw the tanker parked on a small grassy patch behind the garage the next morning I reckoned it was only about 1,200 gallons, say 6,000 litres, that had been delivered. The tanker was only small, about 10 feet long and about 8 feet by 5 feet elliptical in section, the size of an army water bowser. I realised then how lucky we had been in meeting our benefactor, and having thereby gained a ration of this precious fluid.

We were promised five litres by the teacher so on that Friday morning, 31 May, we went down with a petrol can to collect the petrol at the garage. A queue had formed, controlled by a gendarme armed with a pistol but when it was our turn to be served a shock awaited us. The tanker driver, a hero really to my mind, having brought it up from the refineries at Rouen during the previous night, despite enemy air activity which was nearly continuous now with high-level bombers, wanted 100 francs per litre paid in gold. A fortune really and we had no gold – though the French had, because they were said to keep gold coins in their mattresses from time immemorial. A common coin was the gold 'Louis', and there was the 'Napoleon', I think it's name was, both of which were in everyday circulation like sovereigns used to be in England.

This, incidentally, was a lesson in real economics, namely that when paper money or coin becomes valueless or is believed to be valueless, gold is the only universal means of paying for something you must have, something which could well be a matter of life or death, as in our case. The question of gold not earning interest becomes irrelevant, because if you cannot pay for something you must have, you will have problems. Such considerations really clear the mind and concentrate the thoughts if you find yourself in such a situation where money has no value.

However, I did have something nearly as good as gold at the time, which the tanker driver recognised, and this was a British five-pound note, the old-fashioned large white note. This had been folded and sewn in my battledress blouse lining by my mother while I was on my embarkation leave in early 1940 and was another reason why I did not get a new blouse at the depot at Eu. This note I now cut out with my knife and produced with something of a flourish, like a magician producing a rabbit out of a hat. He smiled and put the fiver in his back pocket – to me it implied he thought Britain would not lose, come what may, though if we had lost the War then gold would be have been more valuable for certain transactions than any number of notes, five pound or otherwise. Nevertheless, perhaps one day a British fiver would be useful currency to our friend, the tanker driver, or maybe our schoolteacher benefactor had put a word in for us.

My mother did many useful things for me in her life but I think, with hindsight, this act with the fiver was the most valuable of them all.

He gave us the petrol and we put it in the tank, all five litres of it, paying for it with the whole of the fiver. This would take us to Rouen, and beyond if necessary, maybe 60 or 70 km in total.

We took the bike back to the house of the schoolteacher, said good-bye to him, his wife and his children, which was rather emotional.

To surprise us, at the last minute, when we were ready to go, he said he had written a letter to Geoff's mother in Dewsbury to tell her we had stayed with him and we were OK at that time. This letter eventually got through, by some near miracle of the Franco-British postal services, and Mrs Grimshaw came down to tell my mother I was also OK. Unfortunately Mrs Grimshaw did not keep the letter, something I regret.

He also asked for our opinion as to when he should leave the town with his family. I told him to get the car filled up now with petrol, and ready to go with food, clothing etc. and then, when he saw or heard of the enemy aircraft changing from high-level Heinkels or Dorniers to Stuka dive-bombers then he should go instantly, regardless of whether it was day or night. The teacher had bought fifty litres for 5,000 francs, paid for in gold coin, and said he would be going before the day was out. As we moved off away from the house I could see his wife getting the kids into the car so I expected them to set off very soon without waiting for changes in bombing tactics.

Geoff and I left for Rouen, after this brief moment of emotion with our benefactor's family, and we never heard from them again, though we were both intensely grateful for his efforts on our behalf at what was a difficult period for us.

Our journey into Rouen was uneventful, we just chugged along in the intermittent stream of refugees and when we joined the main road, Neufchatel to Rouen, dropped our speed down to almost walking pace with the rest of the wheeled traffic and people, though being on a motorbike we could nip in and out of the slower, clumsier vehicles.

In due course we overtook a great big hay cart pulled by a big strapping horse as we were nearing Rouen. On top of the hay was a group of ten or twelve British soldiers, and low and behold, they were KOYLIs who let out such a roar of delight when they recognised us as we drew alongside them. They were mostly my old mates and were with the RQMS, who was driving the cart with every sign of competence, and for whom I had worked briefly before I was put in the Intelligence Section with Lieutenant Lee. What a moment it was for me to see them again, after all this time that I had been on the run. I knew then that we were doing the right thing in making for Rouen and the relative safety of an Army reception camp somewhere there because I felt there was no way an RQMS would get it wrong. They said they had been on the road for over a week without seeing any other KOYLIs, so we were no wiser about the fate of our battalion.

Some two hours later we rode across the famous Pont Corneille in Rouen, which wasn't blown until 8 or 9 June, on our way to a reception camp south of the city to where we had been directed by the British Military Police when we first met them north of the city. It was now late in the evening of Friday, 31 May; I had been on the rail and road exactly two weeks, mostly alone, Friday to Friday. It had been a long, arduous and worrying time.

After crossing the bridge over the River Seine we quickly covered the 10 km or so to the camp which was sited at the side of an air base, alongside a big forest. This base was used by the RAF and the French Armee de l'Air, and I would come to know it and its runways very well in the coming days. The first sight, as we drove into the camp, was of a big open-sided marquee in which was sitting a big plump military policeman, a sergeant 'redcap', whose first words, when he saw us on a civilian motorbike, were: 'That's not an Army bike. Where did you purloin it?'

Geoff said, 'In Dieppe, the owner was dead, killed in the bombing, and so didn't need it.'

'OK,' the policeman said, 'you on the bike run it in to the vehicle pool up behind me who will deal with it, while you with the Bren go down to the reception centre on my left to get a meal and a bed.'

I still cannot get over the way the redcap NCO said 'purloin'. He made it sound as if purloin has a connection with 'not guilty' or 'not proven' whereas if he had said 'pinched' or 'stolen' it would have somehow made us feel guilty before being court-martialled.

And that was the last I saw of Geoff for nearly a year, until he happened to come on leave while I was at home in Dewsbury. So Geoff's part in my story ends here without even a goodbye to my old mate of nearly fifteen years; and we were still young lads, not yet twenty years of age.

It was about a year later when I next saw him again and we got very badly drunk on port wine. He told me he surrendered the bike to the camp motor pool as ordered by the redcap, which involved Geoff in all sorts of paperwork because it was a civilian bike. Then by chance he met up with some KOYLIs who were in the process of moving out of the camp at that very moment to set off immediately by rail to somewhere near Rennes, back in Brittany. There was no chance for him or the KOYLIs finding me, somewhere unknown to them, in this big camp and take me along with them, so unfortunately, I was left behind. Of course I didn't know all this at the time and I thought the disappearance of Geoff was one of those wartime things which have no explanation.

So I was left at Rouen with much more excitement to come. I had no money now, no food, no cigarettes and no mates from my own regiment.

It was a bit disconcerting to say the least.

Chapter V

At Rouen

After another good night's sleep, this time in the reception centre at this camp south of Rouen, I got up to find it a beautiful day – Saturday, 1 June – the Glorious First of June of Naval fame which became an important date to my wife and I four years later. This year, 1940, it was very pleasant, sunny and warm, a forecast perhaps of really good weather for now and which hopefully, for we soldiers, would continue during the weeks ahead.

I wandered round the camp looking for KOYLIs but found none. I asked people if they had seen any; I went to the Orderly Room of the camp, going to the front entrance where I had encountered the big Sergeant redcap on my arrival the day before – but I got no joy with any of them. The redcap said my mate and the motorbike must have been directed elsewhere after leaving him as he had not seen him again. He also said that he had seen no KOYLIs come in the camp since our arrival.

So where was Geoff and the party of my old mates on the horse-drawn hay cart we passed the previous day? It was a mystery which I never did fathom until I saw Geoff a year later; now I was on my own again and apparently would have to determine my own salvation as I did after Abbeville a week before. I was becoming anxious, however, as it could be that they had gone to join the remnants of the Battalion, moving off together in some unknown direction, perhaps even further west where they might reform and re-equip. And meanwhile, was I to stay here kicking my heels in frustration and wondering what to do for the best, or what? Indeed, I began to wonder if I was a deserter!

It was disconcerting to be so uncertain over what to do. In a sense I had run out of orders and nobody seemed anxious to give me any now or take any responsibility for my future.

Anyway, leaving the future to the future – it was a lovely day and for some hours I sat at the camp entrance with the redcaps, in the sunshine, watching the poor devils who straggled into camp giving their names, numbers and units. I was still looking out for KOYLIs or 'Dirty Dukes' but saw none come in to reception in all this time. There were plenty of other famous regiments and corps represented by the men straggling in, but seeing the state of most of them I began to realise that there would be many others who wouldn't make it, who wouldn't be straggling anywhere. They would have given up, or become casualties, way back. Maybe the bulk of my Regiment and many of my friends were among these.

I began to realise how fortunate we all were to be at this camp in the circumstances regardless of whether we were wounded or not. It was like seeing the tail-end runners in a marathon race struggling across the winning line. These stragglers were generally shattered, some helping others, many with boots worn out with holes through them and old bits of clothing or rags tied round the soles of their boots to provide some protection to their feet. Some were using rifles as crutches, some were bandaged heavily, and almost all of them were in very poor condition, probably after walking and hobbling from the Somme battle front nearly 100 convoluted miles away. Yet I remember many had a grin on their face when they saw us; some even called out sarcastic remarks aimed at the redcaps and even at me!

It surprised me a little that no attempt that I could see had been made by anyone to send out foraging parties with trucks to pick these men up from the road east of Rouen, bringing them into safety here before they could be taken by the enemy or before their medical condition could have got any worse.

They were all directed to the reception areas, like Geoff and I had been, where I supposed they would be sorted out, given a medical examination, cleaned up, fed and put to bed for at least twenty-four hours' rest.

One particular group of about a dozen badly battered men really caught my eye – they were Royal Engineers. I found out from talking with them that they were part of the same company I had met earlier near Abbeville, and when I talked with these men at Rouen they told me the same story of fighting tanks from the sewers under the streets of Amiens with bundles of dynamite. They attacked the tanks by raising the manhole covers slightly, from below, and rolling the explosives, with a four-second detonator delay, in the direction of a track as the tank approached and then ducking back down the manhole. They reckoned that even if they didn't kill the tank they at least caused the crew to wonder where this powerful explosion had come from. Consequently, they reckoned, the tank crew would have to watch from then on every side street and passageway in future in case more explosive devices came from the same unknown direction, with possibly devastating results for them. But when they told me that as soon as the tank crews realised what was going on they called up their elite specialist infantry shock troops to come after the Royal Engineers in these sewers, armed with their stick grenades and sub-machine-guns, I sensed the horror of it all.

After hours of watching everybody coming in the camp that first day and failing to find any of my mates, not even a 'Dirty Duke' or any of the other Yorkshire regiments, I began to think I was too late, they had indeed been and gone, whether a few or a lot, before we arrived and by some fluke Geoff must have been caught up by the tail end of them, as they were actually moving out on Friday evening at about the time he and I were arriving. This meant I, who hadn't been caught up by the retreating KOYLIs, was on my own so I might as well have a good look round to see the camp's layout before turning in for what might well be my last night's sleep in a real bed.

It appeared my end of the camp was near the end of the main runway of a big military airfield. On one side of the whole camp, so far as I could see, was a very big forest with a minor road running alongside it leading into the camp or base, while on the other side of my little part of the base was a farm with cattle and byres and farm animals with lots of ducks, hens and bantams running around in the farmyard – a really typical bit of French rural farmland with a major military airbase put down beside it. The camp seemed to run away into the forest, up alongside the runway and out of sight with the orderly room a good half a mile away from where I was.

The runway seemed to be on the other side of a corner of the forest, at right angles to our side and the farm, so that it formed a letter L with the camp, the farm and this corner of the forest. The camp was a big one, of many Nissen huts of corrugated iron, which were let into the ground for about two feet. This made the huts a bit damp perhaps but it turned out to be good protection against blast and shrapnel from those bombs which exploded on impact and to which we were to be subjected later. The hut I was in was up near the end of the runway, about 200 yards from it, near where a multiple-barrelled 'pom-pom' was sited, protected by a heavy barricade of sandbags. There were also several machine-gun nests with Lewis guns on either side of the runway and a group of zig-zag slit trenches sited between our huts and the guns.

All in all it was an impressive-looking set-up, though I cannot remember whether the air base had a concrete runway or a grass one, albeit I do seem to remember it had landing lights down the edges. The only snag about it all that I can remember well was that the guns were never manned by regular troops from an AA battery; in the event I and men like me had to man them at very short notice. Luckily, to some extent, some of us knew what we were about.

Anyway, after a quiet day generally prowling around and getting my bearings, I went back to the hut, a talk with the lads there over a mug of cocoa and to bed again. I really was getting concerned now as to what I was going to do – no one in authority seemed to be the slightest bit interested in me.

Next morning, after breakfast, I went up to the entrance again to see who was coming in this Sunday, 2 June. But it was all quiet and some time later the Sergeant went off to what I supposed was the Sergeants' Mess, leaving me temporarily in charge of Reception. It remained quiet, however, no more stragglers came, but after thirty minutes or so the Sergeant returned with good news for me, – he had got me a job, paid too, as an armed guard at a 'Gentleman's Club' down in town. Transport was arranged, there and back, and I was to do a twelve-hour shift with all meals provided and 100 French francs per shift. That was very good pay, as much in a day as I got in a week; there would be some danger of course but in my present circumstances that was a very good offer.

'Get your Bren,' he said, 'fill your mags and report back here as quick as you can.'

So I did just that and was whisked off to this very posh club down on the river bank near the centre of Rouen quite near the big bridges. This well-paid guard job, for a French civilian club, seemed a bit odd at this time for a serviceman like me but as it was arranged by the redcaps I accepted it and was glad of it – at least it gave me a job to do and some badly needed money at the same time.

The club was in a very large old house with a discreet glass entrance opening from the quay at the side of the river, not too far from these big bridges. The door in the entrance led into a large lobby with comfortable chairs, side tables, sofas, and a very impressive glass-fronted office at the rear of the lobby. It had a very high ceiling with ornate plasterwork and beautiful electric chandeliers. On the right were great wide stairs, with elaborate wrought-iron banisters, curving up to the left over the lobby area, while on the ground floor, on the left through a pair of glass swing doors, was a big lounge which led into the club proper with its bars, restaurant and meeting rooms. I remember the 'art nouveau' style of the place and its decorations as if it were yesterday. It was all maroon and cream-coloured walls, flock paper, very old fashioned, and the beautiful chandeliers, very thick carpets, extremely comfortable red leather armchairs and corner sofas made it feel both homely and comfortable. It really was a place of extreme luxury, but no place for a rough infantryman like me!

There was also an unobtrusive service by uniformed waiters of both sexes bearing trays full of drinks, sandwiches and so on. It was all very civilised.

The War seemed to be in another world, except that because of this war I had been engaged, with others I supposed, to guard this place and the occupants against the entry of dangerous undesirables hanging around outside in Rouen, some armed, in uniform or civvies, who might try to enter to loot or rob. My instructions from the Sergeant redcap were simple: disable, or kill if you have to, anyone who may try to force entry against the wishes of the manager, particularly if I thought they were armed.

I had a very comfortable, well-upholstered, upright seat, in front of the office, from where I strolled around from time to time to loosen my muscles and keep my reflexes sharp. Every few hours a waiter would bring me a tray of food, though no alcoholic drinks, with plenty of coffee and we would have a somewhat strained conversation using my then poor French with the waiter and anyone in the office. One such conversation was with a French-Algerian girl about my age who spoke a little English. She told me she was working there so that she could make money for a big dowry and so be able to marry a man of 'good status' back home in Algeria.

It turned out to be a quiet day for me – I think the sight of the Bren gun across my knees, cradled in my arms and obviously ready for action by someone who clearly knew how to use it, put off potential troublemakers who might have entered through the partly frosted glass doors of the club had they not seen me. The Bren is a formidable weapon and at that time I would not have looked at all reassuring in my dirty uniform and steel helmet so fortunately nobody tried anything.

Near midnight I was relieved by another soldier and was returned to camp in the car which had brought him to the club. It was all very efficient, and before I left I was given the 100 francs pay, for which I had to sign. All in all it had been a good day for me and as things were quiet temporarily I was able to do another two days' guard duty on the Monday and Tuesday. It kept me occupied and while I was on guard the redcaps at the camp kept an eye open for any KOYLIs or anyone else who could be useful to me, who might turn up. I was glad to have something to do and it gave me some very useful French currency, but really it was too good to last as I was to discover on Wednesday, 5 June.

Trouble started before we got up – a dawn air raid on our camp caught us just as we were waking at about 0530 hrs and thinking reluctantly about the walk to the ablutions for the daily wash and shave. A newspaper delivery girl was in our hut at this time delivering her papers, mostly French ones though there were one or two English; she also brought bars of chocolate and bags of sweets and gave us the local news in her broken English.

In the midst of this homely domestic scene of the usual haggling over her prices came the sudden whoosh of the first stick of bombs. We heard them coming, one, two, three quite near, but numbers four and five right at the side of our hut. By then we were already out of bed and on the floor, me and my mate from the adjoining bed with the paper girl between us, she screaming her head off and shrapnel tearing through the corrugated steel sides of the hut. We were safe though because we were below ground level by about twenty inches, as the hut was let into the surface of the field. These were impact bombs, probably 250 kilo, judging by the size of the crater, the radius of the blast zone and the subsequent damage. So all the lumps of metal and blast went harmlessly over our heads. Bomb number six exploded nearer the farmyard and then the second and subsequent sticks of bombs criss-crossed the other huts nearby. More sticks straddled other buildings in our part of the big camp causing fires and some casualties while others mashed up the end of the runway and some of the machine-gun nests.

When it all went quiet again, after the planes flew off, we generally rushed around seeing to casualties as best we could with our field dressings until the Medics arrived. Then we grabbed a hastily prepared sandwich, probably of dry bread and cold American bacon, from the nearby dining-room marquee before we dashed off, unshaven and only partly dressed, to the gun positions near the end of the runway and waited for the next attack.

It had been a sudden and violent raid, a warning of more to come I reckoned, so as soon as I got the chance I quickly dressed fully and grabbed some more food while it was still quiet and then returned to the guns via our hut area, inspecting the damage on my way back.

I saw there were six craters across our line of huts, probably five or six parallel Nissen huts, but fortunately no direct hits on any of them but two near misses on our hut with much blast damage such as steel sheets torn off, and shrapnel holes. The craters were shallow, still smoking, a matter of only a few inches deep but about six feet in diameter. There were many lines radiating from the crater through the long grass for a distance of about thirty feet where the shrapnel and bits of bomb casing had ripped along at near ground level before coming to a standstill.

It was rather eerie to examine these after-effects of a raid. I found two fairly large pieces of casing which had come from the last bomb and had exploded on our side of the farmyard. The larger piece had initials on it, big initials in white on grey metal, probably 1½″ high, so there was no chance of being mistaken. It showed 'DC', my initials! I brought this piece home with me but it has since disappeared.

The chap I was with said, 'It's got your initials on it, Nobby.'

'Hell fire,' said I. 'That was a lucky one, I reckon I'll survive now if the one with my name on it has missed me.'

There were a number of chickens sat near the site of a bomb crater on the edge of the farmyard, crouched down; they turned out to be dead, but there were no injuries so I guessed they were killed either by shock or blast. A strange thing was that every chicken was sat on a mess of excrement under their rear end. I wondered about this for a long time, it was a phenomenon I had not previously encountered and I wondered if it applied to humans in similar circumstances. The cows were bellowing and kicking up a devil of a racket but none seemed to be hurt; perhaps they were inside their stable in relative safety being milked or something when the early morning raid began.

Later on, in the middle of the morning, perhaps three or four hours later, there was a second big raid by fighter aircraft – Messerschmitt 109s again, strafing the runway at the far end away from us, shooting up aircraft on the ground, and then coming along over the runway to shoot us up too. It's a devastating experience knowing that these powerfully gunned fast machines are trying to kill you!

In the quiet spell of a minute or so while they turned to realign themselves prior to attacking us again, one of the lads who slept in our hut joined us and ran to the multiple pom-pom and got it ready for firing. I and some of the others ran to man the several Lewis guns in the gun pits and got them ready for action too. Then, when the squadrons of aircraft next flew up the runway at zero altitude a few minutes later towards our position we began firing. The man on the pom-pom must have known what he was doing because 20mm cannon shells streamed out from the four barrels, and we all cheered like mad when one of the Messerschmitts veered off course, bursting into flames as it crashed in the fields away from us. The others, however, all attacked the pom-pom in succesion and it, the gunner and the sandbags all disappeared in clouds of smoke, dust, sand and fire. I reckon he, whoever he was, deserved a medal. Oddly enough, they didn't seem to attack the Lewis gun emplacements in this sweep, all concentrating on the pom-pom area, one after another.

It was all over in a matter of seconds as we watched this really awe-inspiring sight of instant destruction before having to jump for our own lives into the slit trenches when they attacked us on their next pass. After the first attack by several aircraft we realised these slit trenches could be a dangerous place. One leg of the layout was more open to the enemy fire than the other, depending on from which direction the aircraft came. You therefore had to be fully aware of their direction of approach and then be able to get in the right stretch of slit trench at the right moment. Failure to achieve this meant you could be a sitting duck when there were about 2,500 bullets per minute sweeping towards you from a Messerschmitt doing about 300 m.p.h.

Achieving this required that one of you had to position himself at the apex of the zig-zag, with his head above the parapet to watch the enemy, call out how they were coming and then you would all rush into the safer leg to huddle up against the correct wall, i.e. the safer wall, of the trench. I had this job of watching out and calling because I happened to be at the apex, but after a few goes at dodging the persistent enemy fire one of the lads, who was something of a religious nut, a bit of a preacher, cracked and screamed that he couldn't stand this any longer and tried to climb out of the trench near where I was standing. I managed to thump him down to the floor just before the enemy aircraft swept up again and opened fire and so he survived until some of the other lads were able to pinion him and hold him down. My God, he was like a madman in his struggles to escape and I do not think we few could have saved him if the attack had gone on for a few more passes as my calling system was getting out of synchronisation with the attacks. We were lucky and the fighters flew away after another shoot-up, this time wrecking the machine-gun nests completely so now there were no fixed AA defences of any sort at our end of the runway.

And so the day went on with air raids now about every hour, a mixture of high-level bombing raids with Heinkel He111s and low-level fighter strafes with Messerschmitt 109s. Later in the day a flight of RAF Hurricanes followed by some Lysanders took off from a grass airstrip at the side of the main runway, some distance away from us and flew off towards the west, presumably to rebase themselves further back. However, the Luftwaffe didn't attack our huts and the Reception Centre again that day so we had something of a bed to sleep in that night, though we could see the stars through the holes in the sides and top of the hut and through the several places where steel sheets had been torn off.

Thursday, 6 June, was a repeat of the same type of air raids but now they were attacking transport lorries parked for miles at the side of the forest on the minor road referred to earlier. The damage here was very severe with scores of big lorries disabled by damage to lights, windscreens, radiators, tyres and cooling systems apart from those destroyed or burnt out by direct hits or near misses. I saw a RASC mobile workshop unit struggling to repair some of these vehicles in order to get them mobile again and away into the forest out of sight, but it was hopeless really – there were too many trucks to repair with too many jobs on each truck for the few men available. It then occurred to me that maybe I could attach myself to this unit because I wasn't going to find the KOYLIs again and so I ought to get in with somebody like them if I was to have any hope of getting back to England.

While hanging around them for a while to see what was going on I managed to contact an officer, the workshop's lieutenant, to whom I told my story, briefly telling him how I was an apprentice fitter/turner/miller back in civvy street, at Hirst's of Dewsbury, and that I could repair radiators as fast as or faster than his men were able to do. We were able to talk in relative peace as this mobile workshop was sited in a small clearing at the side of the road on the edge of the forest somewhat away from the camp where all the damage was being done. Five or six of their trucks were parked in a semicircle, like a circus, and the crew lived in the trucks. The reception camp, or what was left of it, was on the other side of the road away from us and stretched up the side of the forest towards the airfield. Fires and smoke were everywhere by now and it was pretty obvious this camp and airfield were finished. The mobile workshop looked a better billet for me now than hanging around the wreck of the camp and air base as they were rapidly disappearing as a result of the nearly continuous air raids. And adding to my uncertainty was the awkward fact that I had not the faintest idea where the forward elements of the enemy were, although from their use of fighters and dive-bombers I knew they must be near.

The Lieutenant consulted with his workshops sergeant as to whether they could add a supernumerary like me to their strength and decided they could, but only if I could pass a trade test, I suppose, to check my story. So, the Sergeant took me in the mobile workshop lorry to test me on their lathe and set me the task. To me it was a piece of cake, making a 2″ screw and nut from a bit of bright round bar for the screw and a bit of black hexagonal bar for the nut. The lathe was a brand new 'Colchester' tool-room lathe, 6″ centres or thereabouts, and I was making a beautiful job of his test piece. I had set the lead screw up on the lathe to cut a six-threads-per-inch screw as he had asked me to do. I prepared the cutting tools for the job, internal and external threads, turning the blank for the screw test piece using a micrometer to get the size accurate to plus nothing minus 1/1000 inch. The test piece would be worth 100 per cent I reckoned and I would be in.

Then suddenly the workshops officer stopped the test, and said, 'That's enough, I can see you know what you are doing.' With that he and his workshop sergeant major gave me an oral exam lasting about half an hour. I passed that and the officer said,

'OK, you're in, get helping the men on the lorries with radiator repairs.'

Not only that but he marked my pay book there and then that I had been trade tested and graded as a 'Turner, Grade 2' RASC and signed his name and unit with the date and my new rate of pay. This, as you will read later, became very, very useful when back in England I applied for release on Class A reserve. So, after a bit of messing about and form filling I was temporarily attached to a RASC mobile workshop. Marvellous!

I now worked all the hours of daylight repairing radiators; we cut out the damaged finned area, plugged and brazed all the open water passages to restore the water circulation, replaced any damaged water hoses, replaced any damaged electrics and thermostats, filled the engine with water, oil and petrol, checked the tyres and we were off. This went on for two days up to Saturday, 8 June. As fast as we repaired the trucks they were driven away into the forest to hide them, prior to rejoining RASC units. A minority got caught in the continuing air raids but on the whole we were doing fairly well.

Unknown to us, however, the German forces were getting ever nearer to Rouen and were now in the northern suburbs engaged in street fighting with the French. A desperate battle was also going on to the south-east of Rouen on the right bank of the river near Elbeuf and Rouvray, very near to us, when we were ordered to move west to another safer part of the forest some few miles away from the fighting, to hide our precious lorries which we were repairing. They were big vehicles, about 20-tonners had they been civilian rated, and I guess we had about thirty of them. We moved by night and by early Sunday morning we were nice and snug, parked alongside forest tracks under a fairly dense canopy of leaves.

Some of the men had been fitting circular AA mountings on the cab roofs of some of the trucks during these last few days. These were now fitted with Lewis guns; quite impressive they looked too, but now a fatal urge to fire the guns at some enemy target took hold of these men. They wanted to have a go, to take on the first aircraft that appeared, having been on the receiving end of German air attacks for several days they wanted revenge.

This, however, was the worst possible time for us to go attacking German aircraft – the Germans were fighting in Rouen itself and were trying to cross the River Seine upstream of Rouen and therefore we would be exposed to immediate dive-bomber counter attacks if we gave our position away by futile aggressive action. Despite my pleas to the workshop sergeant not to attack, and I was much more experienced in these matters than he, when a Stork observation plane flew over our area of the forest they opened fire with the Lewis guns. It was fairly low, maybe 1,000 feet, but the Stork could turn on a sixpence, and they didn't hit it. It rapidly flew off, to the derisive cheers of my new companions. I told them we must get out while we still had time, as it would be necessary to manoeuvre these big lorries in complicated U-turns on the slippery forest tracks where they had parked them, but they wouldn't listen.

Within a very short period of time, squadrons of dive-bombers attacked our part of the forest. It was chaos, with fires from the emergency petrol dumps, lorries hit and destroyed, and men running all over the area away from the site pinpointed by the Stork when it had been fired at. I and some others were working near the edge of the affected area and were in a good position to escape, so we dashed off down a forest track and soon put a quarter of a mile between us and the attack zone and found shelter behind some rocks, a kind of escarpment, on the edge of a small hollow. We stayed there until the bombers left and then returned to a scene of real destruction. Most of the big lorries were burned out with their loads, along with some of our workshop transports. The petrol bowsers were gone and many of the men were wounded with a few killed. It had been a very expensive lesson for them.

Those needing medical treatment, probably a quarter of the men, were sent off to a military hospital which was still functioning at the other side of the reception camp area nearer Rouen where at least they would be seen to before the Germans took over later in the day, or the next day and we survivors pushed off in about five trucks that were left, including the workshop lorry, making our way a few miles further to the west. Sunday, 9 June saw the big bridges of Rouen blown and much of the resistance on the right bank of the River Seine ceased. We in our few surviving trucks, moved still further away from this area and made camp, sleeping in the lorries, in another forest near the town of Bourgtheroulde, about 20 km south-west of Rouen.

I was now with a motorised unit of sorts so there would, I hoped, be no more walking for me. But where we were going?

I had no cigarettes, there was little food except a few tins of ship's biscuits and bully beef and we hadn't petrol for more than 100 miles. The outlook was not good, but I had most of my 300 francs from the club so there was hope!

Chapter VI

Rouen to the South-West Coast of Brittany

WE HAD TURNED up a track off the main road late at night in the enormous forest near Bourgtheroulde and made camp there because this area seemed to be still peaceful. As it remained fairly quiet the next day we stayed on well into the morning of what was Monday, 10 June in order to get a good night's rest followed by a substantial breakfast made up from the remainder of our rations. We thought we might as well take it easy for a little while and eat up as there was no knowing what lay ahead of us nor when we would next get a meal in these increasingly difficult times.

The workshops officer went off to Movement Control for petrol and movement orders and came back some time later with authority to pick up a small two-wheeled trailer petrol bowser at a depot near Bernay. This was further south-west, probably 20 miles via Brionne, say an hour's travelling normally. Things were not normal, however, on the main roads with all the refugees and some military traffic going in our direction to the south-west and even more masses of military traffic – guns, trucks and tank transporters – going in the other direction. Conditions in these circumstances were chaotic, massive traffic jams at all the crossroads and junctions, the ever-present likelihood of air attack from the usual clear blue sky, and no sign of the RAF or the French Armee de l'Air.

The journey took all day, a dreadful journey in fits and starts, and it was very late in the evening when we pulled into the depot at

Bernay, too late to do much before morning, too late to get any food, so it was a good job we'd had a decent meal before we started our journey as we got nothing else that day.

Next morning, very early, we were in the petrol dump to collect the bowser with its 1,000 gallons of petrol, a most valuable commodity for our future as we were going to need this for our trucks to keep them going. Also, though we didn't know it then, we would need some of the petrol to barter in order to get food and cigarettes in the next week or so.

I also got a surprise as a result of this call at the petrol dump, when the workshops officer received orders to find a guard to escort a bus which was coming in shortly. The bus was travelling from Rouen to Argentan, with a party of about fifty very well-connected girls, of eighteen or nineteen years of age, from a Roman Catholic boarding school. They had already encounted trouble from marauding groups on the loose between Rouen and Bernay attempting to steal some of their jewellry and their escorts of two or three nuns could not cope with problems of this nature.

Our workshop unit was also going on to Argentan, as ordered by Movement Control, so it was considered we could conveniently find a guard. We had also heard rumours that our unit was to meet up with more British troops coming in from Cherbourg to reinforce the remainder of the British Expeditionary Force left in France after Dunkirk. This was going to form a 2nd BEF and would include a Canadian Armoured Division, another British Armoured Division, part of which was already in France, and several British Motorised Infantry Divisions, plus the 150,000 men remaining in France from the 1st BEF. These forces, when added to the remains of the French Home armies and the several armies of French colonial troops from the French colonies, would constitute a force superior to those already lost in the mayhem up to and after Dunkirk.

As we were already 'en route' to Argentan, Movement Control

reckoned we could find a guard for this special bus. The guard would escort the bus to an Argentan rendezvous with our workshops unit later in the day when the guard would leave the bus and hopefully rejoin the workshop. The bus would then take the girls to their new school in Argentan. A nice little job the petrol dump officer said, as reported by our workshops officer, and some very influential French people would be extremely grateful.

The workshops officer came back with this tale, looked at me and said, 'You'll do, Clark. You are an infantryman and you will have done guard duty like this before. The RTO at Argentan will direct you to where we will be; we'll be waiting for you because we will not be moving off until tomorrow.'

But, I wondered, what would happen to me if events prevented them from waiting for me, if they were ordered to move on in a hurry, before I reached them? Would I join up with some other unit of this Second Expeditionary Force in Argantan, say some other infantry regiment, or what? It was all rather disquieting, but orders were orders and so I had to get on with it.

So in no time at all I was getting on the special bus and it drove off, following after the last of our unit vehicles, which we soon lost because of the chaotic traffic and because they, perhaps, took a different route. The bus was a long one, a single-decker tour-type bus, being driven by an efficient-looking nun with two other nuns sat at the front of the bus. There were about fifty girls in it dressed in civvy clothes, very smart-looking, pretty French girls and I could visualise how they would attract men of all types, all ages, good and bad, whose imaginations, when they were faced by all these pretty girls in these circumstances, would run riot. So I could foresee possible trouble at this time when law and order was progressively breaking down as civil authority slowly collapsed, however temporarily, due to the effects of the War.

At first I sat on a seat near the front with the Bren across my knee, rather like a shotgun guard on a 'Wild West' stagecoach. But after an hour or so of this in the slow moving bus, which kept stopping and starting because of all the traffic, I thought it would be awkward for me, sat like that, if trouble started. And in any case it made me a sitting-duck target for any aggressor, and so obvious to any determined attackers. Also, I wouldn't have as clear a field of fire as I would prefer. I might even hit one of the girls which would be a catastrophe for all of us.

So I decided to get down on the floor, nearer the rear of the bus, and stand the Bren on its front bipod thereby giving me a clear firm view up the centre of the bus to the front via the fairly wide aisle between the seats. Then I would be able to shoot, if I had to, any troublemaker who might have got on board without him being aware until the last moment that I was there waiting for him, although unfortunately I would almost inevitably shatter the windscreen in the process. On the other hand, it would be easier for the nuns and the girls to keep clear of the aisle, which was to be my line of sight, at those times when danger seemed likely. But I'd also have to see who was at the other side of the windscreen before firing or I might hit someone by mistake. It was all a bit cramped for good, accurate shooting, so I sincerely hoped it would not come to that.

Some hours later, we came to a small town where the senior nun stopped the bus, perhaps unwisely, to let some of our passengers get off to use the toilets in the centre of the town. Then we set off again but had to stop quite soon, after travelling less than a quarter of a mile, because of unexpected worsening traffic jams and crowds of refugees in the streets.

A party of colonial troops who were walking past, with rifles over their shoulders appeared, three or four of them, with black shiny faces and red tarbooshs, probably Senegalese, and before anyone could stop him one of them made to get on the bus. The others walked on past, seemingly oblivious of his action, leaving him alone on the steps by the door which he then opened. I don't think any of these men had seen me on the floor, and no one in the bus made a sound – I think they were petrified with fear of the possible consequences.

The man came through the door and came into the centre of the bus, at the front, up near the driver, with a great grin on his face, as bold as brass. The bus was halted by the milling throng and the traffic ahead of us; it was all very still with the engine quietly idling. The intruder was a young man and perhaps his mind was full of dreams and fancies, of macho deeds of masculinity rather than stealing jewellry, when, without warning he suddenly saw me as he turned his head to look down the bus. There, right in front of him, was a dirty machine-gunner in a camouflage-netted steel helmet about twenty feet away who had him dead to rights – and who was waiting for him.

He was looking straight down the flash eliminator and barrel of a machine-gun. Before he could move I put the safety catch off, with its awe-inspiring metallic click in that dead silent bus, and he knew he faced decision time. His jaw dropped, his grin disappeared and he seemed to age ten years in a moment. His skin went grey from its previous shiny black as we faced each other for a second or two before I broke the tension with the command: *'Allez vous en, vitement, vitement.'*

He almost fell off the bus and as I got to my feet to watch him go, with the Bren cradled in my arms, ready to fire at the slightest sign of reaction from either him or his pals, I watched him run after his mates, and all of them disappeared out of sight down a side street with his mates gesticulating at him with apparent annoyance as they went.

But I don't know who was the more relieved – me or the African. All I know was that if I had to fire I would and damn the consequences. I've often thought about this incident and in the early years after the War I was sure I would have opened fire, despite the confines of the bus, if I were pushed by circumstances. I had, at this time, a great sense of chivalry towards women and girls. And if they or their honour were attacked and I was in a position to stop the attack, I would do so, regardless.

However, the colonials were gone and without wasting any time the nun driver put the bus in gear, the other nuns smiled with relief – nuns have such beatific smiles – and within seconds we were off again. This time there were to be no more stops for anything until we got to Argentan and safety some hours later.

Strangely enough, I got the feeling the girls were as apprehensive about me as they were about the Senegalese soldiers, perhaps they thought I too could be a psychopath and I had a machine-gun, which made it worse. Whatever the reason, I got no thanks for escorting them and I was glad to leave the bus when we got to Argentan town centre. The bus stopped at the railway station to drop me off and I quickly found the RTO in his office on the forecourt. Through him and his directions I had no real difficulty getting back to the workshop unit with its trucks parked up a side street nearby.

So for me it was a case of 'and so to bed', as if nothing had happened, though I was relieved to have found the workshop so easily in this very busy town, and I was thankful no shooting had taken place in defence of my charges. But I was glad to get a simple meal of sorts, haversack rations I think, and then get in my blanket roll and off to sleep on my usual spot on the floor of the workshop lorry. Life as usual once more.

Next day, Wednesday, 12 June, we were up and about early, hoping to make a start on our next move which we hoped would take us into the new army, the new 2nd BEF, when we hoped to get some better food than that we had endured recently. We had been told that some of their units would be moving through Argentan from Cherbourg or the Atlantic ports back towards the Rouen area. But there were no orders along these lines for us about a 2nd BEF rendezvous from either the RTO or Movement Control, so we waited and waited somewhat impatiently.

Well after breakfast, perhaps in mid-morning, we were rewarded by a first sight of units of this new army. They were Canadian artillery units, probably 25-pounders, with ammunition limbers, armoured tractors and logistic trucks, all extremely efficient looking, all newly painted in camouflage-dappled khaki, all brand new. There must have been twenty to thirty pieces of artillery, very impressive looking. These were some of the elements of the much talked about Canadian Armoured Division, and to our amazement they had great banners hanging from the tractors which were towing the guns, proclaiming this to all who could read English. There was no sign of any security, to hide who they were or what was going on from the Germans or their spies; they even had banners saying 'Hitler here we come' hanging across the fronts of the trucks.

When they saw us, parked there ready to move off in the opposite direction to them, they went bananas, shouting to ask why we were moving in the opposite direction to them. Why were we retreating like this? They wanted to know where we had left the remainder of our vehicles, where were the tanks, the artillery and so on. It was embarassing; oh yes, in their eyes we were a crowd of bums, who were leaving it all to the Canadians. They were moving fast, probably 25 miles an hour, with motorcycle outriders and were soon out of sight on their way to Rouen in something of a cloud of dust as there was not much traffic now heading in their direction.

We kept on waiting for orders all day but there was nothing doing, the workshops officer kept chasing Movement Control and the RTO for news but all to no avail as there was nothing for us. Late in the evening, before it was dark, however, and while we were still waiting, we suddenly got one hell of a surprise. The Canadians came back, going even faster in the opposite direction, i.e. in our direction, but this time without either the guns or the ammunition limbers. The banners had been taken down and when we shouted to ask them where Hitler was there wasn't any reply – they hadn't a word for the cat and we never saw them again.

This was amazing, quite incredible in fact, and we all wondered what on earth had happened further on to the east. They had obviously been recalled by someone high up, but who and why? With fifty years of hindsight it begins to look to me as if the prolonged wait all day by us for our movement orders and the turn around of the enthusiastic Canadian unit were linked. There must have been a major U-turn high up in London at this time to cause all this, plus a lot more troop movements in all probability that we were unaware of.

The next morning, Thursday, 13 June, we finally received our movement order to go to Alencon, which was about 50 km to the south of Argentan via the town of Sees. The road was already busy again with civilian and military traffic in both directions and there was some minor enemy air activity at Sees. This was a major road junction, and when we got near there we were delayed a bit as a result of the raids. However we arrived at Alencon late in the evening and were directed by the Movement Control people to a position out of town, which was on the edge of a nearby forest, for our own safety, I thought, as severe bombing was expected in this area now the Germans had begun to attack Normandy in a big way. We had a quiet night, however, though we heard bombers flying overhead most of the time attacking units to the north of us.

Friday, 14 June, and we were very short of both food and cigarettes, the latter being the most important for morale, despite what ASH and others may say now. The workshops officer decided to try to obtain both by bartering some of our petrol – he reckoned he could afford to sacrifice a quarter of the petrol in the bowser, 200 gallons say, for supplies of food and cigs to keep us going for a few days.

So before setting off for our next stop, Laval, as per Movement

Control orders, he decided to go shopping. He and his sergeant came back some time later with about 100 cigarettes per man plus packs of tea, sugar, dried milk, iron rations, dozens of tins of American cooked bacon, dozens of tins of bully beef and packs of thick naval ship's biscuits, which I knew from past experience were as hard as rocks. It sounds a lot but when you reckon it is to feed a group of thirty or more ravenous soldiers for a week it gets into proportion, particularly when you realise they haven't had a real meal for several days.

Other dramatic incidents around this time were all to do with trying to get more food after the above seemingly generous rations ran out. Included in these activities was a break-in at what we thought was an abandoned French Army food store way out in the country which we had passed on our way to make an overnight camp. After making camp and eating our supper of a few miserable ship's biscuits and a slice of bully beef, we decided to return to the assumed food store. We reached it without any difficulty, even though it was dark and fairly late at night, and made a recce to confirm no one was on guard. It was all quiet and abandoned, so we decided to break in.

We broke into the end wall of a big store-type building, the end wall being at the side of a minor road with only a narrow strip of gravel between the wall and the tarmac of the road. We positioned the truck across the road and carefully reversed with a jabbing motion into the wall using the jib end projecting beyond the rear of the workshops truck as a battering ram. We then backed the truck right up against the end wall, enlarged the resulting small hole we had made by the jib end ram to larger than tea-chest size, and then got into the building. You could say it was an early type of 'ram raid', so common nowadays. It had the advantage for us that the truck was able to back right up against the end wall and so hide what we were doing as no one could see us inside the truck, working away on the broken wall in near silence.

Once inside the store we dragged cases of unknown contents up to the crane hook hanging from the jib, now projecting inside the building, and lifted them into the truck with the pulley blocks. Noisy rattling things they were too; we thought they would wake everyone up in the area, but no one seemed to be alerted. Then back to our camp we went, a few miles away, before we were seen.

Back at camp we jemmied the cases open, with our mouths watering at the thoughts of the big meal we were anticipating could now be cooked for us, only to find that the total contents of the hard-won cases of stolen goods were merely thousands of tins of Heinz beans, and not the tins of corned beef or bacon or fancy French Army food we were dreaming of. So disappointed were we that we went back to the store for a second time, disregarding the risks of our earlier break-in having been discovered, and opened two or three more cases on the floor of the building before going to the trouble of getting them into the truck. But all we found were more beans. It must have been a Heinz beans store. I often wondered what the storemen or guards of this place thought when they discovered the mess we had made. We made a meal of the beans, though; they were not too bad, considering, and they were a bit of a change for us.

We also went on a 'rabbit shoot' during one idle afternoon, but soon found you couldn't do much in the catering line with a rabbit which had been hit by a .303! We even had thoughts of butchering some of the young sheep we came across – the thought of leg of lamb was enticing, but we hadn't a butcher among our number so this was a rather reluctant non-starter. Indeed, at this period in our journey, which we realised was towards the west, we were becoming more and more obsessed with food and cigarettes, or the lack of them. We wondered most of the time when would we get some relief from this hunger – such things, for example, as a real meal of meat and three veg followed by a 20-pack of Players Navy Cut or Capstan full strength!

Activity by the enemy was slight in the area we were slowly passing through, making numerous diversions and detours so as to avoid, we assumed, populous areas from where we could have been reported on to the enemy. It was, on the whole, a peaceful journey, enemy action being concentrated more to the north, well away from us, so we had nothing to distract us from our rather selfish thoughts of enticing meals. It was nevertheless a long journey – I reckoned the total mileage of all our to-ing and fro-ing must have amounted to about 450 km or more from Rouen to St Nazaire.

Events had now become rather confused as to time, date and place. Movements seemed a bit haphazard – we would go for an hour or so and then stop for half a day – orders seemed few and far between and we got no food or any chance to engage in a bit of barter. We didn't see anyone, either British or French, civvy or soldier. The idea of going home to England seemed remote and we began to accept that we would never make it; we were forgotten, would be left behind and would inevitably finish up marching off to a German prison camp in the east.

Eventually, quite unexpectedly and certainly without any warning or advance notice from anyone, we reached a huge almost abandoned air base and depot which seemed to have been used as a receiving store for supplies coming in from America. This depot was to the north-east of St Nazaire, the big French naval base on the Atlantic coast in the west of Brittany, north-west of the city of Nantes. Once we arrived it was obvious that this was our final destination – we had reached our Shangri-La.

It was in the evening of Saturday, 15 June when we arrived there. The date is firmly fixed in my mind by the sinking, only two days later, of the Cunarder *Lancastria* which went down on the afternoon of 17 June, just off the port, with what was officially said to be 5,000 men on board. We were told later, some days later, that we were supposed to have sailed on this liner from St Nazaire but we arrived in the docks or at the quay far too late to do this and the liner sailed without us. It did, however, take every man who could get to it via shuttle craft in the time available, regardless of the numbers involved, and we were told that in total nearly 8,000 men boarded the liner before it sailed. It was, I believe, standing room only.

In fact, when we did eventually get to the quay, having been delayed by one of the biggest air raids I had experienced, the liner was long gone and was indeed sunk some miles away to the north-west along with some of the escorting warships. Also sunk were some of the other boats, British and French, which came to rescue survivors. I reckon there were well over 8,000 men in total on all these sunken ships as no account would be taken of numbers when the men were getting aboard or being rescued later.

These events fix the date of our arrival at the depot near St Nazaire. Despite getting more and more hungry and with no cigarettes on this seemingly endless journey, directed by Movement Control, we did eventually reach our target – this enormous Allied camp, arms dump and airbase, seemingly set up to receive food, munitions, trucks, tanks and guns from the USA in anticipation of a long war. It was now late in the evening of Saturday, 15 June. and we were immediately given cigarettes by the NAAFI, which was still operating, though not for much longer, and some American chocolate – Hershey bars I think they were called.

So we went to bed happy, eating, drinking tea, smoking and lying in a proper bed in this, to us, most wonderful camp. At long last we had got the meal we had been dreaming about for nearly a week. Life seemed much more rosy, and without doubt we were going home. So, we reckoned, we had not been forgotten after all.

Next day, Sunday, 16 June, turned out to be a day of unremitting hard work after our several recent days of idleness. And what work as we, a mobile workshop of thirty or forty men, who were normally employed in repairing vehicles, were put to work wrecking them as efficiently and quickly as we could. There were hundreds of trucks on which we spent what seemed to be hours of back-breaking labour with sledge-hammers, smashing engine generators, starters, plugs, distributors – anything that looked as if it would be damaged by a good clout with a sledgehammer, such as the dashboard with all its switches, and so on. Eventually, after a few hours of this, and I have no recollection of seeing either our workshops officer or the warrant officer during this time, someone said let's drain the oil out of the engines and then run them at full speed until the engines seize up. It sounded a bit drastic but we tried it and this method worked a treat, though some of the engines seemed to be in no hurry to seize up. Then someone said, 'Let's drive some of the trucks over to the edge of the airbase, on the grass out of harm's way, and then set them on fire by dousing them with petrol.' So this was tried, but rejected after a few were dealt with in this way because it was a bit too dangerous for us. So most of us went back to running the engines with no oil to the point of seizure, though a few liked the fire method despite its risks and a few drained all the water from the radiator and ran the engines until this too caused seizure.

We continued with this work until it was dark, always waiting for news about the ships which we had been promised were coming to St Nazaire, some miles away, to pick us up. But news of their arrival never seemed to reach us and we began to get moods of depression again, with a growing feeling we were not going to get away no matter what morale-lifting rumours were put about by the camp authorities.

Some of the men found a real treasure trove later that evening. They found what could have been a NAAFI train of five or six wagons filled with cases of whisky, brandy, spirits in some of the wagons, and army issue rum in glass carboys, packed in straw, in other wagons. All these spirits were dangerous stimulants to us in our present circumstances, waiting for boats that were promised but which never seemed to come and with enemy formations somewhere behind us drawing nearer. But, in no time at all, a dozen men were drinking the spirits, particularly the rum, and rapidly becoming blind drunk, shouting, cursing, fighting and generally behaving stupidly which was alarming when some of the participants were armed.

An officer, a stranger whom I had not seen before, tried to check this behaviour by ordering them to stop, but it was all in vain and getting annoyed by the insults he received he started waving his pistol about and trying to shout louder than the noise being made by the men he was trying to control. They ignored him and kicked up more noise than ever, getting more and more aggressive and insulting. It seemed as if the situation would turn nasty but I managed to get him to come away to one side, out of earshot of the men, and told him the best way to clear the wagons was to craftily set the rum-sodden straw on fire, without letting anyone see it being done. The drunks would think one of them had done it while smoking a cigarette and in a matter of minutes there would be a raging fire consuming everything and keeping the drunks away from the mess and the liquor.

'By God,' he said, 'that's the answer.'

Carefully and quietly we two lowered one of the smallish side doors on the flat rum wagon which by now was full of rum-soaked straw; there were some broken glass carboys of rum and a few drunks fighting in the unholy mess were getting cut from broken glass in the process.

We quietly lit the edge of the straw with the officer's cigarette lighter and 'whoosh', it exploded into flames, as if it were a petrol fire. It was the biggest Christmas pudding ceremony I have ever seen! We were almost knocked over in the rush out of that flaming wagon. Now we had started something we could neither control nor stop, and quickly several other flat trucks filled with spirits were on fire.

And that wasn't the end of it, the fire spread to neighbouring closed wagons which unknown to us were filled with wooden boxes of small arms ammunition, all wrapped in oiled paper and in oil-soaked boxes; this went up like a torch as well, with multiple explosions from the burning ammunition.

It was a most dramatic fire and dangerous too, because in the dark of that evening it could attract any enemy bombers which may be prowling around. Still, it was one way of getting rid of stores to stop them falling into enemy hands. There was no way of putting the fire out and as it was confined to only a dozen railway trucks or less, standing well clear of any other wagons or buildings, we let it burn itself out.

Shortly after this episode, I and a gunner came across a number of four-barrelled electrically controlled pom-poms in a hanger. They were equipped with small motor/generator sets to power the movement of the multiple-barrel AA units, moving in both elevation and direction, with their 20-mm magazines for each barrel. There was a central seat with a control panel in front of it and an electrically illuminated sighting system of concentric circles on a clear perspex screen through which you saw the target quite clearly. It was American, a beautiful weapon and we itched to try it out somewhere. There were also associated tractor units and ammunition limbers – a beautiful set-up and several of them were all fuelled up and ready to go.

So we coupled up a tractor unit and towed one of the 'super' guns to near the main entrance where we parked on the grass about 100 feet back from the gates. It was dark of course by now, and the other lads were starting their supper as we got the motor going, set the outriggers out from the gun and had some fun with traversing and aiming. We fired off a few rounds into a wood at the side in order to check stability, that is a few rounds from each of the four barrels, which was really exciting. The results on the wood were devastating. My, what a weapon!

We played around a bit more, traversing and firing, then decided to call it a day and go for some supper – when we heard the dreaded noise of heavy caterpillars coming up the tarmac road towards the camp entrance where we were. It was a heavy tank from the sound of it, and soon it came into sight about 100 yards away, round a gentle curve in the road down from the camp entrance. I was already sat on the seat between the four barrels of the gun, the generator was running, power was on, so without thinking I traversed the weapon in seconds and lined up the circular sights, illuminated on the perspex screen, on the front of the oncoming tank and pressed the triggers to open continuous fire with all four barrels.

By now the tank was probably only 200 feet away and to me there was no question that it was an enemy. I had no hesitation in firing, the rule there at that time was that 'He who shoots first and hits survives'. Indeed, I could not have run away if I had wanted to, as the tank was too near for me to have any hope of escaping before I would have been shot. I held the triggers down for several seconds and watched with some satisfaction as four streams of 20-mm shells hit, exploded, made fire, smoke, ricocheted and whined off into the dark in a great blaze of sparks, light, flame and fumes. It was tremendous, the tank stopped dead as most of the shells had struck the front where the driver was and some could well have penetrated the vision slit or periscope, to his 'disadvantage', as the lawyers say.

Then to our surprise two teenagers, a boy and a girl, jumped out of the cupola, hands above their heads, and climbed down the side of the tank, which we could now see clearly was not German, as there were no Nazi crosses on the sides. How they missed being killed I don't know – I suppose you could say they were joyriders, but it had not been much joy for them as they were trembling like aspen leaves from the shock of these few seconds of extreme violence.

They seemed to be alright, the tank armour would have protected them really, so we left them to find their own way home, wherever that was, and went back for our delayed supper, very thankful that the tank had not been German and not the point tank of an advancing German column.

When we got in the canteen it was to hear one of the officers giving us all our marching orders – we were to get our kit together and fall in at the front of the canteen in fifteen minutes time bringing with us what food and cigarettes we could carry. He said we had to be prepared for a seven-or eight-mile march, lasting two hours perhaps, a hint not to bring too much weight. So about 100 of us, some not entirely sober and some whose mates had tried rather unsuccessfully to sober them up after the fires on the two trains of ammunition and spirits, lined up and set off for St Nazaire.

I suspect a few of the paralytic drunks from the rum booze-up were left behind, lying dead to the world in some warm bed in a quiet corner of the base, because no one had been able to knock any sense into them or waken them up. Tomorrow, sadly, when they woke up, they would be on their own, waiting to be taken by the Germans who were now expected to be following up rapidly behind us.

We set off walking informally in threes, feeling we ought to be singing 'It's a long way to Tipperary', but this soon became a single file as we straggled rather than walked down the twisting country lanes turning into posh residential roads in the early hours of the morning. It was probably about 2 a.m., after a fairly hectic day starting with wrecking trucks, setting a drunken orgy on fire, getting an AA gun to work and killing a suspected enemy tank.

We reached the St Nazaire industrial area after an hour or so and were making our way through a conglomeration of railway lines, factories, sheds and threading our way carefully round railway trucks and signal boxes. We were on our way to the docks, where we had been told the long-awaited Cunard liner *Lancastria* would be waiting for us, though the area did seem to be deserted which was rather disquieting. Suddenly the air raid sirens sounded and before you could draw breath, bombs were dropping among us, right among us. A full-scale raid had started on the docks where we now were and we scattered in all directions. I dived under a line of rail wagons – there were several parked trains in the yard – as I reckoned this would be one of the safest places to be if I used a wagon as an air raid shelter.

How wrong can you be! This was one of the most violent and sudden raids I had been in since leaving Rennes weeks before and it went on for perhaps twenty minutes of nearly non-stop bombing, with many near misses as rail trucks were blown up in the midst of the marshalling yard and industrial area in sudden enormous blazes of brilliant golden light, crashing back again on other trucks in a mass of crumpled metal. Groups of men, perhaps only fifty feet away from me, would be hit and would appear in one of these great bomb flashes with bodies tossed in the air like rag dolls. I cowered under the railway truck I had selected for its supposedly air raid sheltering qualities, scratching a shallow trench in the ballast of granite stones between the sleepers and the lines in a desperate effort to maximise the cover beside me and to gain the most sideways protection from the railway lines on either side.

For the first time I began to feel real fear after all these weeks of wartime activity when I had felt no fear and no apprehension, and for the first time I was hit. It was only a slight wound but it created a nasty gash on my knee and of course could have been worse, much worse. The wound would be large enough to justify three or four stitches in normal circumstances, though not out here. It also created a slight graze on the left side of my nose; it could have torn my knee cap off and taken out my left eye had it been an inch deeper, or had I been lying slightly differently.

All this was caused by a great lump of the steel casing from a bomb, which had exploded on our train of wagons about two wagons away from me. It, and a lot more shrapnel, whistled up under the train between the rail bed and the underside of the wagons and this piece hit me as I lay on my side between the lines. It made a shallow tear through my trousers and the skin covering my knee cap, went on to touch the side of my nose, and tipped the edge of my steel helmet which was towards the back of my head because of the way I was lying on the ground. The blow on my helmet rim gave me a hell of a shock, the chin strap tightened up under my jaw as the helmet kicked back, almost choking me, and the lump of bomb casing ricocheted into the man sheltering behind me about a yard or two further on. I heard the dull thud as it hit him, somewhere in the stomach region, followed by a low groan and then silence. One way and another I really felt, for the first time, that I would not get out of this situation. I think I called, in vain, for stretcher bearers to cope with the man behind me and then I dealt with my knee.

I bandaged my wound with my first-aid dressing as best I could in this awkward cramped position, lying on my side, and at the first opportunity moved away from the railway depot or marshalling yard or whatever it was and got to a quay where I found a few other men were sheltering.

There I was told, to my absolute horror, that the *Lancastria* had sailed many hours before taking everybody who was in the docks, leaving no one except us – and while this loading was going on, with eventually the liner sailing, we were still at the air base and stores depot miles away fighting over rum, having a last supper, and shooting up a supposed enemy tank.

Dawn came, I think it was Tuesday, 18 June and a total of perhaps fifty or sixty soldiers huddled together on the quay and wondered what on earth we were going to do. Later that morning a civvy came to tell us that the liner *Lancastria* had been sunk further to the north-west when it was on its way to England with the loss of several

The sinking of the Lancastria, *17 June 1940*
(By kind permission of the National Maritime Museum)

thousand lives – and then I realised how lucky we had been not to be on it despite all appearances to the contrary. There was some desultory talk about the War being effectively over for us and when we heard later from another Frenchman that the 'traitor' de Gaulle had flown to England from Bordeaux we knew we would have to do something decisive soon as the war here in France was over.

The Frenchman said he had heard this on French State Radio, TSF, and that it had also reported on the news that a new government, led by Marshal Pétain, the victor of Verdun in the First World War, had been formed by the parliamentary deputies sitting at Bordeaux and was forthwith to seek a ceasefire from the Germans. In the eyes of the French people we were eventually able to talk to this was similar to the recent change of Prime Minister in England from Chamberlain to Churchill under similar circumstances of defeat, i.e. Norway.

In such an atmosphere of doubt and even suspicion it was difficult to know where the truth lay but eventually one of our number, who was French speaking, was able to hear another French news bulletin on the TSF and reported back to us, saying, 'The war is finishing over here, de Gaulle has flown to England, Pétain is boss man now, we are stuck at St Nazaire and there is no boat for us here.'

Someone suggested we return to the camp we left the previous night and form a mobile column with a few towed multiple pom-poms, supply trucks, petrol and water bowsers, make our way down the coast towards Spain as fast as possible and crash the frontier if we had to. There was some argument about this scheme but a small majority hoped for a direct escape to England from this area of France, even though there were no boats. I, and the other infantry types fancied our chances in a run to Spain with a mobile column and on to neutral Portugal, a run of perhaps twenty-four hours non-stop for a column of the type envisaged.

We eventually agreed to return to the camp, take some of the remaining trucks with petrol, water and food, and make our way south on coast roads, without any maps, and see what we could find by way of small boats escaping to England – a good compromise scheme to see what small boats we could find first and only crash the frontier if we had no choice. And in all this time spent in St Nazaire, I cannot remember seeing more than a handful of civilians – it was like Dieppe again.

So this was what we did, starting off in the late morning of, I think, Wednesday, 19 June (my date is based on the dates of events concerning de Gaulle and the formation of Pétain's government) heading south with about five big trucks well stocked with food, cigs, weapons, ammo and towing bowsers of fuel and water, but no multiple AA guns, i.e. no offensive heavy weapons. Our intention was to see if we could find boats from ports to the south of St Nazaire before the Germans and French began to round up parties like ours. And if we did not find any boats taking refugees to Britain then we would eventually and inevitably crash the frontier into Spain.

We hadn't much time left as the Panzers were near Nantes at this time so we would have to get across the Loire river as quickly as possible or else we would be cut off and going nowhere except to a prisoner-of-war camp.

Chapter VII

The Return to England from the Atlantic Coast of France

AT THE END of Chapter VI I said I dated our movements at St Nazaire by reference to General de Gaulle and Marshal Pétain and dates concerning them. I said that while I was a bit uncertain as to some of the earlier dates in our escape from Rouen, eventually leading up nearly two weeks later to our arrival at St Nazaire, I was pretty sure we moved off from St Nazaire in the late morning of Wednesday, 19 June. So, how was I so sure of this date when I had been somewhat vague earlier?

During the early hours of the dawn, probably at about 6 a.m., after the night-time air raid on the dock area of St Nazaire when I was hit and we were in a state of some confusion, with no officers leading us as I remember, and me with a bleeding knee under a rough bandage, we spoke with a French civilian. He understood a bit of English, and told us that the traitor de Gaulle – his words – had fled to England from Bordeaux the day before. He also told us that the Cunard liner *Lancastria* had been sunk.

According to Churchill's book *The Second World War*, vol. 3, *The Fall of France*, Churchill says, and I cannot do better than quote him verbatim:

> So that very morning – the 17th – de Gaulle went to his office in Bordeaux, made a number of engagements for the afternoon as a blind, and then drove to the airfield with his friend Spears to see him off. They shook hands and said good-bye and as the plane began to move

> de Gaulle stepped in and slammed the door. The machine soared off into the air, while the French police and officials gaped.

Earlier, in the same book, Churchill says, referring to the second BEF evacuation:

> At Brest and the western ports the evacuations were numerous. The German air attack on the transports was heavy. One frightful incident occurred on the 17th at St. Nazaire. The 20,000 ton liner *Lancastria*, with about five thousand men on board, was bombed just as she was about to leave. Upwards of three thousand men perished. The rest were rescued under continued air attack by the devotion of the small craft, and it was some time before the knowledge became public.

Thus Churchill gives two references to the 17th and both occurred while we were waiting for the move down to the quay at St Nazaire to board the *Lancastria.*

It was that next day, the 18th, in the dock area, after the bombing, that the civilian told us of both events, adding that he had heard of them on the radio TSF. He also told us that Marshal Pétain had been elected Head of State and was going to seek an armistice after taking advice from General Weygand, the French Commander-in-Chief.

Hence our move south, the following morning, must have been on the 19th; we were now getting very near the signing of the armistice. One of our lads, who spoke French, also heard this news on the TSF – he called it 'Tay-Ess-Eff' – and confirmed the story to us. The gap of a day between these messages from the TSF and our moving off to the south, plus our finding a boat sailing to England, is a blank to me but I know we spent a considerable time arguing and discussing what we were going to do. You must remember we had no officers with us and I don't even remember any sergeants being present to lead our consideration of these serious matters. We were just a bunch of ordinary blokes in what was an unprecedented situation.

I cannot remember details of this journey south, the name of the boat, the harbour or quay from which we sailed, nevertheless I do remember very clearly the type of boat it was and certain details of the quay. I also remember vividly a very emotional incident with a party of Jews as we were getting ready to embark. I can recall so well the voice of our French-speaking mate saying 'Tay-Ess-Eff' as he told us earlier in the day all the important news that he had heard on the radio regarding de Gaulle and Pétain.

We took five or six lorries from those remaining at the base which we had not had the time to smash up and travelled down the coast. I would guess it was 30 miles or so before we came to this small harbour with one short quay where there were two British officers. They were dressed in beautifully creased barathea dress uniforms and highly polished brown leather Sam Brownes, boots and revolver holsters. Very smart they were, a credit to the British Army, as they stood with their swagger sticks under their left arms. These were the first British officers we had seen for some time, their smart dress and their manner boosted our morale no end, an example I never forgot.

They stood beside a small gangplank attached to a boat tied up at the quay. It was a small coaster type of boat, not a smelly fishing boat, more of an old-fashioned tramp steamer, maybe 120 feet long with a deadweight of perhaps 500 tons. On the foredeck were about fifty ragged soldiers looking at us as we pulled off the main road, which went on further to the south towards La Rochelle, and drove on to this little quay. It was evening and approaching sunset, very tranquil and as peaceful a setting as you could hope to find in these times.

The officers asked who we were, where we were from and where were we trying to get to and then told us that this boat was sailing to England that evening after it got dark, as soon as they were absolutely sure no more stragglers would be coming along hoping to be picked up. After having our pay books checked by Military Police who were also standing by the gangplank, they said we could come with them, if we wanted, as the land war in France was to all intents and purposes over. They also said that as far as they knew this would be the last boat for England from this part of France. 'Come with us,' they said, 'and take your chance on this boat or go on down south to Spain if you must but with no guarantee of a trip to England and your homes from down there.'

We decided to join the boat and so a group of some twenty of us, including me, began to push our lorries over the edge of the quay into the sea while the others joined the groups of other soldiers on the foredeck, pretty well filling up all the remaining open deck space. Other men had already filled the holds below the decks so on the whole the boat was now full.

While all this was going on, and I was one of the few soldiers still on the quay dealing with the last of our lorries, a number of Jewish families came to the boat, in cars, and we saw that each family comprised several adults with children and teenagers. Many had brought a rabbi with them, or we assumed they were rabbis because of their odd little skull caps; one of whom spoke with the officers in English, and demanded places for all his people on the boat. The senior officer, a major I think, asked if they were British citizens and on being told they were not he said he could not let them board. They then demanded 'sanctuary' on British territory because if they stayed in France they said they would eventually be killed by the Nazis. They said the Major must let them board this boat or he would be answerable for the consequences later as this was said to be the last boat sailing away from this part of France, therefore this boat was their last chance of escape to safety.

There was quite a crowd milling round the Major by now, angry and shouting, after the rabbi, who was doing the talking, told the others in their own language, which was not French, what had been said. But the Major stuck to his guns, repeating that his orders were that only British citizens with passports or other proof of their nationality could come aboard this ship.

The atmosphere got so heated that he called for some of the Military Police, who were already on the boat, to stand guard at the foot of the gangplank with batons and rifles to prevent any unauthorised persons from gaining entry to the boat. On seeing this the Jews moved away a little distance and went into a huddle to talk over what had been said. After this impromptu conference, the rabbi, who spoke very good English, returned to the Major and made him an offer, which they must have presumed was too good or too generous to be refused.

The offer was that any soldier who would marry, on the quay here and now before a Rabbi, one of the young girls would receive a dowry of a thousand pounds sterling, in gold, and he would also receive financial assistance for himself and his bride from relatives of the bride in England, assuming that the bride was taken with her new husband on this boat to England.

I listened to all this as it was being said, and found it was quite incredible. Generous, perhaps, in some ways, but who would marry some strange foreign girl in this fashion – it really was a measure of the desperation of these people who could send their child off like this.

The Major said, 'No way can we do this: these troops are under military law in a foreign country and therefore cannot marry anyone without a full investigation being made in England to establish that there are no hindrances to the marriage and then the man's Commanding Officer must give his consent. Where they are now in France, on this quay, it is not possible to carry out any such investigation. Furthermore, they have no Regimental Commanding Officer here to authorise any such marriage and I certainly cannot undertake any such action for them. I am sorry but such a solution to your problem is impossible.'

The rabbi went back to report this to his people, whereupon they slowly and rather reluctantly moved back to the cars and drove away to the south without another word.

It was all rather sad, and with this conclusion to what had been a very emotional experience, I went up the gangplank with my few mates, who had been working on shore with me dumping the lorries, leaving the darkening quay deserted. The crew cast off, letting the ropes fall back in the water though still tied to the bollards, and we sailed off into the darkness, or as they say in the films, we sailed off into the sunset – literally – a moment of really great emotion.

It was, I am sure, late in the evening of Wednesday, 19 June as not only does this agree with dates arrived at via Churchill but it will also agree in later chapters with the important dates of my eventual homecoming in England.

I found a little area on the foredeck out of any draughts, behind the steel bulwark running round the bow to form the prow, on which I bedded down with my single blanket forming a simple bed, with my back pack filled with clothing as a pillow. This small area became my niche for the next six days up to the Tuesday of the following week where I stood, leaned, watched the sea, slept at night and prepared my basically simple meals of biscuits, bully beef and chocolate iron rations, washed down with a mug of tea twice a day.

Meals were simple because there was no food of any form on this boat except the bit reserved for the few crew members. The only food other than that was the bits and pieces we had left from our looting of the stores back at the base near St Nazaire, which was carried on our backs, along with the cigarettes, some light clothing and spare ammunition for the Bren, which I still had. It was all self-catering on this cruise! All they could give us were mugs of tea, twice a day, without milk.

There were no cigarettes on the boat either, though I had obtained about 1,200 Players from the NAAFI at the St Nazaire base before we left it. From the stores there, I also got a few days' ration of ship's biscuits and bully beef. It was all there was but it was good nourishing food. Again I felt a bit like Robinson Crusoe except this time I was not alone as he was.

The next day, Thursday, we spent all day in a state of high alert, with AA defences of several Lewis guns and Bren guns on makeshift mountings manned all the time. It was another beautiful day of blue skies and brilliant sunshine and though we were sailing west at full speed, perhaps 10 knots, we were continually aware of the threat from enemy air activity when we were so near the coast. We did not begin to relax and feel reasonably safe until we had steamed 250 miles or so away from France.

All this day we sailed due west and when the next day came, Friday, 21 June, we continued in the same westerly direction. The day was uneventful, and after another night of thin sleep on this cold, hard, unyielding fore deck we awoke on the Saturday to find ourselves still sailing west. This continued until about midday, and stories had begun to spread that we were going to North America, either the USA or Canada, and we all began to brighten up at the mere thought of it and the famed hospitality we would receive!

But regrettably this euphoria could not last with our daydreams of being received in New York or Halifax, and during Saturday afternoon to our great disappointment we turned right and from the position of the sun corresponding to the time of day we knew we were going north. This continued for about fifteen hours, through the late evening and during the darkness of Saturday night, but early on Sunday morning we turned right again, stopping all the developing speculation that we were going to Northern Ireland. We were now going east, and we maintained this course throughout Sunday and Monday so the amateur navigators among us had now worked out that we must be nearing Land's End and by the next day we would be somewhere near either Plymouth or Bristol.

They were right – Tuesday, 25 June saw us sail into Plymouth Sound and dock at the quay near the foot of Plymouth Hoe at about 10 a.m. to a tumultuous reception.

There was all the hooting and sirens from the many ships in harbour and the shouting and cheering of an enormous crowd, numbering many thousands on the Hoe. Through this vast crowd we hundred or so ragged, hungry and wounded soldiers marched. I say hundred or so deliberately because the majority on our ship, which we were told was indeed the last ship out of France, were Military Police numbering perhaps 200 men.

They were the cause of something of a hostile demonstration in the harbour as we were coming in to the Hoe to land when they put on their previously hidden red caps. These had not been worn on the boat during the journey from France, which had begun nearly a week before, so we had no idea who they were and they hadn't mixed with any of us so far as I know.

They then massed on the forecastle deck space, where I had been sleeping rough for the last six nights, as a solid red phalanx at the front of thc boat and pushed us ordinary squaddies out of our usual positions and down into the centre of the boat. When the soldiers round the harbour side and all the thousands of sailors on the warships saw this sudden flash of red, as the MPs put on their red caps, a sudden roar of anger surged from the massed audience all round the docks, and echoed back from the hills, amplifying the sound to many times its original volume. I would think the whole of the city heard it and wondered what on earth was going on!

'Chuck 'em in't sea, chuck 'em overboard, the b ...... s.'

They meant it too, and now we realised why the two Officers were so smart in their dress uniforms and shining leather at the quay in France – they too were coppers. There was a quick order from one of the their officers and immediately all the red caps were doused. The boat tied up only temporarily at the quay, near the Hoe, and we ordinary squaddies were immediately disembarked, about a hundred of us as I've said, all scruffy, dirty, unshaven like tramps and the boat backed off as quick as possible and went in the direction of the naval base to the west.

We who had disembarked from the boat were formed up in the usual files of threes and marched up the hill where there were thousands of women waiting for us. The women lined the two sides of the narrow corridor which had been formed through which we would have to march. Just after we started our march from the quay, on our way up this hill, a car or a lorry backfired with two or three loud explosions. It says something about the state of our reflexes as the column of threes immediately broke up and we scattered to the sides of the road and the shelter of the nearby buildings as a reaction to the imagined explosions of mortars. We sheepishly reformed our ranks and set off with embarassed grins, but we could not get through the ranks of the women very easily, even with the best efforts of our NCOs who were trying in vain to keep us marching non-stop to the station. The women wanted to kiss us, to give us chocolate, cigarettes and sandwiches while so many wanted to know if we had seen their husbands, sons and boyfriends while on our way to the coast in France.

They held out photographs of their missing loved ones and pleaded with us for news. It was a harrowing, unbelievably sad and grief-stricken struggle for us to get through them up to the station. I could only mumble that I was Light Infantry and say that if the missing man was not in my Regiment or in my Division, the 46th, there was not much chance I would have seen him.

Some of these women had come to Plymouth, after hearing that our boat would be the last one to dock, from all over the south of England, hoping and praying for news; it was a sort of last chance for them. When they knew we hadn't seen anyone resembling the man on the photo held up for our inspection they knew for certain their man was probably missing for ever, with all that would mean for them in the future.

It was indeed extremely emotional.

We eventually reached the station where a train was waiting for us, with food counters and tea urns set up on our platform by the women of the Red Cross who gave us more sandwiches, cake and mugs of tea. In minutes we were on this special train, doors slammed and we were off, but we didn't know where to and we didn't care really either, we were home!

Anyway, suddenly feeling as if all my energy was running out of my body, I put my Bren gun, without its magazine which I kept with me in my web equipment, in the luggage rack and relaxed for the first time in weeks. It was Tuesday morning, about 12 o'clock, 25 June, I was back in England and though I felt relieved I was not elated. I was just exhausted when I thought of all that had happened in recent weeks, my knee was still stiff and awkward even though it was properly bandaged now and beginning to heal.

Life would never be the same again for me, never, I was a surviver!

Chapter VIII

Plymouth to Dewsbury

After the tremendous reception given us by the enormous crowds at Plymouth, we all expected the army authorities to be in a similar generous mood and that we would be sent home on leave within a matter of hours. We hoped that as soon as we had been checked in at some local reception centre, paid and given travel warrants and leave passes, we would be off, even if it meant travel on a night train. But this was not to be as we were soon to find out.

Our train was one of the new open carriage types fitted with tables with seats for four people round each table where we sat and told one another of our experiences. Most of the men I talked with had suffered difficult times, though I seemed to be unique in losing my battalion! I also had a sore nose where it had been grazed at St Nazaire by the bomb fragment, even though this had happened nearly a week before, but in contrast, my knee which was a much more serious gash, was giving no trouble at all. Strange.

We had a tremendous amount of food to eat, sandwiches, pork pies, scones, Cornish pasties, and so on, given us by these women who had come to Plymouth to seek our help in finding their men. There was even a tin of salmon and a loaf of bread with a pack of butter. The women seemed genuinely touched by our poor state, dirty and torn uniforms and bandaged injuries, and we really did appreciate their efforts on our behalf.

The cut on my left knee was healing well but the field dressing was still there making my knee look worse than it really was with its yellow-coloured antiseptic impregnating the khaki bandage showing through the great hole in my trouser leg.

The train was comfortable enough however, the food was good being mostly home made and in due course officers came round to tell us we were being sent to a centre at Mansfield where we would be screened, processed and sent on to holding units. From there we would be sent on leave after being given 48-hour passes. After this short leave we would be absorbed into the front-line forces, via our regiments, with whom we would then await the expected invasion of Britain from Continental Europe.

How long would all this take, when would we be home, we all wanted to know somewhat anxiously, particularly the married men and those few with families – but there was no answer forthcoming to that. So we continued on our way to Mansfield, travelling fast on the special non-stop train, where we arrived in the late afternoon and were taken on to a barracks there by trucks.

It was then a case of a quick superficial check on identity followed by a surrender of weapons to the armoury, a bath, a clean bandage on my knee after it was seen by a docter, and a new uniform to which we transferred our BEF and divisional badges. Following all this was a good solid meal of liver and onions, potatoes and cabbage followed by prunes and custard with endless mugs of tea in a modern 'art deco'-looking Co-op restaurant in the middle of Mansfield.

So, replete at last, we then looked forward to a quick start that evening on the essential admin we knew we had to go through before we could be sent home – but that admin was not to be that day. It was a case of getting a bed space, followed by an hour or so in the canteen talking over the events of recent weeks with a pint of beer in our hand.

I met a very interesting bloke there, a man in his early thirties, who had been fighting in the International Brigade in Spain for two years. He was an Irishman who had been at this centre in Mansfield for some days after he returned to England on his way back to London from Spain and France. He said he wanted to join the British Army now, with a commission but he wasn't being offered one despite his claims of being a colonel in the International Brigade. He said he had papers to prove his claims but they were not being accepted for some reason.

I heard later he was being sent back to Ireland, after I was told he had refused to sign up in the ranks of the British Army prior to being commissioned. It seemed he didn't want to sign up as a private on the basis that he would soon be considered for a commission once he was in. Seemingly he didn't trust us to honour any such bargain, maybe as a consequence of his experiences in Spain, and seemingly we were not so desperate for his services, despite all our losses. A strange but true story, with a bit of uncertainty on both sides.

The next day, Wednesday, 26 June was much more active and perhaps more nerve-wracking for us lone soldiers, with no units to vouch for us. We had to describe our military movements in France with a civilian. He was one of the many who were there, who could well have been a police or M16 official, a grey man about forty, who wanted to know literally every detail of what we had done, why we had done it, places, dates and so on, making us repeat the answers over and over – it was almost like we imagined the German Gestapo would behave.

Eventually he OK'd me and passed me to others in this administration procedure who again wanted to know all my details to pass on to regimental records, War Office and so on. Finally, there was a kit inspection prior to the stores making up our shortages, which in my case were considerable. They included my rifle, which I abandoned in France in order to take a Bren LMG and a gas mask which with my other pieces of personal anti-gas equipment I had abandoned to be able to take up extra bandoleers of ammunition for the Bren. I reckoned I was more likely to need extra Bren gun ammunition than I was to need protective equipment against a theoretical gas attack which was not likely to be made, and there was a limit, after all, to how much I could carry and still retain my mobility.

The Bren and some of the ammunition I had originally, plus two Bren magazines and a spare barrel were brought back by me from France and given, with some pride I may add, to the armoury at Mansfield.

So I had some settling up to do and in addition I had not been properly paid for six weeks. I reckoned that if I got credit for the Bren and the extra ammunition for it, plus my pay, I would be due anything up to fifty or sixty quid, even if they gave me nothing for the fiver I used for petrol and charged me in full for all the missing kit, including the rifle and the gas mask.

In the event I only received one pound advance pay at Mansfield and they told me a final settlement would be made when I got to the KOYLI depot at Strensall to where my final AF 1064, which was my kit statement, would be sent in due course.

These formalities took most of the day and in the evening I attended a boxing match for the army area championships, in all weights from heavyweight down to bantamweight. I enjoyed that match as it took my mind off the thoughts swirling round my head after the day's events, particularly the Gestapo-type questioning. It was also my last evening with some of my new mates, such as the Irishman who went away the next day and wasn't seen again by any of us.

The next day, Thursday, 27 June, was much more interesting for me. I got the impression that the previous day's long-winded security check was somehow connected with what happened that day, as if I had been given a clearance, because I was introduced to two new special formations being created in the Army arising from recent events in France.

The first formation was that of special secret task forces called 'Leopard' Brigade Groups, referred to by Churchill in Vol. 3 of his book *The Second World War*, page 254, when he writes:

> The safety of the country depends on having a large number (now only nine, but should soon be fifteen) of 'Leopard' brigade groups which can be directed swiftly i.e., within four hours, to the points of lodgement.

Churchill was of course referring to a special anti-invasion force. Recruitment of men for these groups was under way by the time I reached Mansfield and, as a member of the Light Infantry with some limited battle experience in France, I was eventually offered a posting to a training unit for these 'Leopards'. I was told it would be at Portsmouth and we were to stay in civilian lodgings in civvy clothes when we were in this country and be paid at a special rate of three pounds a week. We wore uniforms of course when we went on operations. I said I was interested in joining one of these units and so I was interviewed at length by a senior NCO from one of the groups, a recruiting sergeant I supposed. When he was satisfied that I was physically and mentally suitable for the rather onerous duties that would be put upon members of the 'Leopards', we discussed at length the training programme, the types of operations we were to undertake and so on. It seemed that the work was not quite as restricted as Churchill suggested.

We were to go back to France, making landings by small parties from submarines to surprise, attack, terrorise and generally create fear in the minds of German guards wherever they could be found in lonely and relatively isolated positions near the coast. So we were not to be exclusively engaged on defensive work against the Germans after they landed here as described by Churchill, but were perhaps predominently, to be engaged in offensive operations.

Some such attacks had already been made, and the NCO showed me a finger he had taken in one such raid very recently – cut off a

German who was in the process of climbing into a bunker just captured by the 'Leopards'. So it was a rather rough outfit, but it seemed to be very well equipped and organised.

I agreed to a transfer to this new unit because three pounds a week plus civvy digs, and also civvy clothes, when we were in this country, was a very good offer when one was already in the Army and in the Light Infantry at that. As the man in Chicago said when speaking of some activity by the Mafia – the offer was too good to refuse!

All this occupied the morning, ending about noon when a party of us were then taken to Barton air base near Manchester where we watched a training session of the newly set-up parachutists who were jumping from a tethered balloon flying at a height of what was said to be 1,000 feet. An officer of this new formation told us about their duties, their equipment, their type of operations, the type of men they were seeking and so on. But I didn't buy this one as I thought that after the men landed from the air they could be too dependent on other units coming up to support them. They were also dependent on heavy packs of stores and equipment being dropped with them. But what would happen if they could not find these packs after landing, or if they fell into enemy hands? The parachutists couldn't carry sufficient food, weapons and ammunition to last more than a few days and hence they would have to be relieved by someone else if that were possible – and if it were not possible?

In contrast, the 'Leopards' would be much more self-sufficient as they were not jumping out of an aeroplane and possibly landing miles from their target and miles from their stores – they were being put ashore near their objective with loads of essential food and ammunition to back them up.

So for me, the result of this fairly active day of interviews and the trip to Barton was: Yes to the 'Leopards' and No to the Paratroops.

I was told I would be contacted later about being transferred to

Portsmouth – but I regret to say I never was. As a result, I thought the 'Leopard' project had been cancelled and it was not until I read Churchill's book nearly fifty years later that I realised I had probably simply been overlooked in the speed of events at that time.

The next day, Friday, 28 June, was the day when I left Mansfield in mid-morning by train for Sheffield, feeling a bit bemused by all the events of the last two days. When would I be sent home for a brief leave and when would I get back to the KOYLI? I wanted to rejoin the 2/4th Battalion which I had left, or lost, weeks before at Abbeville and of which the only sighting I had made since had been the RQMS and a dozen or so of his men on the horse-drawn hay cart near Rouen. I also wondered when I would get paid – and what about the transfer to Portsmouth to start training with the 'Leopards'?

On arrival at Sheffield Midland station, I reported to the RTO and was taken to a barracks near the centre of the city, south of the main road to Penistone, Barnsley and Dewsbury. So, I reckoned, by fair means or foul, I would be in Dewsbury tomorrow. But, and it was a big but, I had very little money and the Army were not being very generous in this respect.

To get money I decided to try and sell some cigarettes, say 800 Players out of my stock remaining from those I got at the base near St Nazaire, and so late on Friday afternoon I took to the streets near the barracks to try and sell some to passers-by. I sold a few packets but not enough really as I hoped to get two pounds in cash for my cigarettes, but before I got anywhere near that I was stopped by a plain-clothes detective to whom I had been reported by one of the passers-by at the nearby police station. The detective asked me for an explanation and after hearing my story took me to a nearby police canteen where he and I sold the lot now he was convinced they had not been stolen! So now I had the money to get me to Dewsbury on the bus the next day, which was my birthday, and to pay for a few rounds of drinks in the army canteen.

Next morning was a good day in more ways than one, the sun was shining, a really lovely day again, and after breakfast I was called to the Orderly Room. To my delight I was given a 48-hour leave pass and ration allowance, and sent on my way to Dewsbury which I reached in about two hours on the Yorkshire Traction bus from Sheffield to Bradford via Barnsley and Dewsbury. No one took any notice of me, I was just a soldier on leave to them. Any idea that I was coming home from the BEF never seemed to enter their heads, even though I wore the BEF symbols on my epaulettes and the symbol of the 46th Infantry Division on my arms, which was very striking – a mature oak tree on a green background – and was sewn on both arms of my battledress blouse up near the shoulders.

This uncaring attitude towards the BEF and particularly towards the 2nd BEF with its 130,000 men came to haunt me ever more strongly as I had been in both Expeditionary Forces. So had all of those in 2/4th KOYLI and many other northern regiments, and as a result I began to be convinced that the general mass of the population was never going to have much understanding of what had really gone on. I was disappointed by it all and even began to wonder whether it had all been worth it!

Had they heard of the battles on the Somme, Lower Seine and Normandy in 1940? Indeed, had they ever heard of the French forces at Cherbourg who held up the Panzer Corps of General Rommel for forty-eight hours of destruction and killing round Cherbourg? This had no purpose other than to effect the escape from Cherbourg harbour of over 35,000 men of the 2nd BEF which included the remnants of my battalion, 2/4th KOYLI. I did not think it was truly appreciated and events thereafter rather corroborated this opinion for me.

I arrived home at 56 Longcauseway feeling weary, haggard and hungry again at about noon to be met by the news that Mother had gone that very morning to Aunt Mary's at Holmfirth, near Huddersfield. She had gone, I think, to seek consolation from her regarding my being posted 'Missing, believed killed'; of all the Clarks, and at this time she had no blood relatives, Mother was closest to Mary, my father's sister.

Mother had received a telegram conveying condolences for her loss from King George VI that morning and it was all too much for her. For her this was a repeat of 1917 when her brother George was killed and later in the 1930s when her husband, my father, died as a result of being gassed in the First World War in 1917 and 1918, causing him to suffer fifteen years of sickness with endless visits to various hospitals before he finally succumbed.

And Mother got no pension for either of these losses, she got nothing. No wonder she was sickened when I joined the Territorials twenty years after the end of the First World War which had cost her so dear.

My sister Irene went out to phone Aunt Mary to tell Mother that I was home, in one piece. My aunt was married to a wealthy man and was one of the few people to have a phone in those days. So Mother returned, by car I think, as Aunt Mary had a Humber limousine and driver, and there followed, with her, my one and only emotional homecoming. During the evening my mother and I went to see Mrs Grimshaw, Geoff's mum, to tell her of the adventures of Geoff and I, and for me to hear the good news, which my mother already knew, that Geoff was back OK, having returned about ten days previously.

This day, Saturday, 29 June, was my twentieth birthday – although I can't remember any presents or cards or anything special for it to welcome me home. But it was my birthday and it is a date you do not forget, and coincidently it was also the day I got home from France, in one piece.

And that was all there was to it, a return from the dead, a great big anti-climax in a way, though it would have been so very different had I not returned. In which case I would not be writing this now, would I?

Chapter IX

And Finally, my Return Home on Class A Reserve

I RETURNED TO SHEFFIELD on Sunday evening, on the Yorkshire Traction bus again, and was back in the barracks by about 8 p.m., just in time for another liver and onion supper, a drink in the canteen and after cleaning my belt, buttons and boots I was away to bed.

The next day, Monday, 1 July, I received orders to go to the KOYLI depot at Strensall, near York, by train, where I was to wait and wait and wait for five weeks or more with nothing useful to do. I didn't understand this delay at the time but now over fifty years later I wonder whether it was tied up with my application to join the 'Leopard' training unit at Portsmouth. If this had become mixed up with my return to KOYLI and so I had fallen between two units, KOYLI and 'Leopard', I was going nowhere until it was sorted out.

We'll never know now, will we?

So, I reported at Strensall in the afternoon and the first words of my reception by the desk sergeant in the Orderly Room, when he looked at me were:'Get them BEF badges off, there's no b . . . y BEF here. And cut them Divisional badges off an' all. And when you've done that come back here and show me – do it now and give me the b . . . y badges – think on.'

So I went behind the Orderly Room and did what he said. The BEF letters were embroided in navy blue, as I recall, on tubes of khaki fabric which slid over the epaulets on my shoulders and were easy to remove but the Divisional badge was embroidered on stiff fabric about two inches square sewn on each sleeve and had to be cut off by my clasp knife. I then reported back to him, giving him the badges as requested. This again is something I resent up to this day as I have never been able to replace these badges, despite going to many military fairs in the hope of finding new ones.

What a reception this was!

He then checked my identity, checked my movement order and gave me a hut to go to, a Nissen hut, not a dormitory in a proper barrack block. In there were several strays like myself, who seemed to be waiting like Godot in the Russian story for something which never seemed to turn up. They included two particular blokes I palled up with. One was, or said he had been, a chauffeur in France to a general. Who the general was I never asked, and the other was, or again said he had been, a movie photographer, a supposedly good press cameraman called Keene who alleged he had worked for Pathe. He had also been in France, taking movies, but now no one seemed to want him. He said he was waiting for a posting or transfer to a new propaganda unit allegedly being formed in London. But when I finally left Strensall weeks later he was still there, so whether he finally got his posting to film work I never did find out.

Life there was dreadfully boring once I had been checked for kit shortages after my AF 1064, I think it is, came through from records. This confirmed that when I had got back to England and checked in at Mansfield I had been short of a rifle, gas mask, gas equipment, greatcoat and various other items of small kit. All this was to be paid for, with no allowance for the Bren or anything else.

When I protested about this I was told that only the return of the Bren had saved me from being put on the very serious charge of losing a rifle! But I would still have to pay for it, about twelve pounds sterling it was. This, with the cost of the other missing items and taking into account the pay I hadn't received, meant that I owed them 10 pounds or more in final settlement. In the event, rather than argue and lose, as was inevitable in those days, and having had it dragging out for long enough, I borrowed the money from Mother and paid it off quickly. And forgot it.

Nothing seemed to happen regarding a move to either Portsmouth or back to 2/4th KOYLI and whenever I made enquiries I was told to be patient, they said my time would come or words to that effect.

I also had my trade testing and the subsequent small increase in pay revoked as from the date when I went on board the ship to leave France.

But that was to be a blessing in disguise, when after two or three weeks of standstill, as it were, I saw an Army Council Instruction in the Orderly Room. This instruction, which I believe was the highest general command the Army had, said that owing to the war situation and the desperate lack of weapons in the forces, it was necessary to employ every possible man skilled in the highly technical and scarce engineering trades of centre lathe turner, miller, toolmaker, press toolmaker and so on in the manufacture of munitions immediately.

Therefore, all men with such skills, who were apprentice trained, and who were not being employed on work in the Army utilising their skills, must be released from the Army immediately their credentials could be checked with their previous employer or technical college.

This was me to a Tee – an apprentice in my last year of training, I was a turner and toolmaker, had been in attendance at Dewsbury and Huddersfield Technical Colleges for 4½ years part-time tuition and had a brilliant academic record there. And I had just had my army trade testing as a turner, and associated trade pay, revoked so quite obviously the Army did not want to employ me in these trades.

I wrote to my mother that same night to ask her to go to see, immediately, my old employers, A. Hirst & Son Ltd on Bradford Road, to see Mr Bridgeman of Dewsbury Technical College and to also see Dr Ward of Huddersfield Technical College. She was to warn them that the Army would be on to them very soon in connection with this special release scheme under which I was hoping to be released on Class A Reserve to go back to work temporarily in munitions.

I was in the Orderly Room the very next day to fill in the necessary forms to the obvious consternation of the permanent staff, and away the forms went for urgent action.

I expected a reply within a week, because once I had decided on a certain course of action I always wanted quick movement and the sooner the better. But again it wasn't to be as quick as that and week followed week as still nothing happened.

So, hoping to find out what was holding things up back in Dewsbury, I put in for weekend leave, filling it in with the normal leave passes on the Friday without giving it a second thought – and I got it back, all signed and shipshape. Off I went to Dewsbury on the Saturday to see my old employers, Hirsts, and found them in a desperate state wanting all the skilled labour possible with none available at the labour exchange.

They had already filled in all the necessary forms for my release, sent to them by the National Service Officer at the Labour Exchange, and were anxiously awaiting results.

But when I returned to Strensall a real shock awaited me – immediate arrest and banged in the guardroom, locked up on the Sunday night for being 'Absent without leave'. It appeared I shouldn't have gone on weekend leave with what was in effect only a 24-hour pass. They told me with evident relish that I would be up before the Company Commander in the morning and he would remand me for Commanding Officer's Orders in the afternoon where I should certainly get at least two weeks in the cells cleaning pans, because – blah blah blah – I was continuously causing trouble.

Next day, standing to rigid attention in front of the Company Commander in his office and hearing the charges being read out –

absent – I sensed a sudden flutter in the Orderly Room next door, whereupon the Chief Clerk came in and whispered in the officer's ear. Then the Company Commander said words to the effect that:

'Mr Clark, and you are Mr Clark now, I am very sorry about all this, these charges are all struck out as your release to Class A Reserve has come through with effect from Saturday midnight, the time when your 24-hour pass expired. You therefore have no charges to answer.'

Me, Mr Clark again, it was unbelievable, and just in the nick of time too!

It was a case of all hands on deck for the staff of the Orderly Room as they all rushed round to get me off the depot as fast as possible. A truck was laid on to run me down to the station at York for the train to Leeds, I think a haversack ration was thrust in my hands as I went out of the gate and I was off. No demob suit, no farewell party – nothing, just go, with no regrets on my part!

I got in one of the 2nd class smoking carriages near the barrier, put my kit bag in the rack, sat well back with my feet up on the seat opposite, lit a cigarette and relaxed.

You lucky devil, Clark, your luck is still there. Ah, the sudden peace of it all, broken by guards' whistles, steam blowing from the engine and then, just before the train moved off, another soldier, in a new battledress uniform, scrambled into the carriage. He put his kit bag in the rack, turned round and sat down, looking out of the window.

I looked at him, only slightly interested and then my mouth opened in amazement – it was the RSM – my old acquaintance, once my old boss. After a moment of reflection, on realising who he was, looking at this very smart and handsome man of about forty years of age, who previously had always been in the barathea uniform he had been so proud of, I plucked up courage to speak.

'What's happened, Sir?'

He looked up and recognised me as the young soldier from the

RQMS stores who'd measured up all the rooms for him in the various requisitioned hotels and big houses in Wakefield when he needed accommodation for over 300 extra men. He replied, rather bitterly,

'I was accused of weak leadership and lack of moral fibre, which was proven to their satisfaction. I have been discharged and am being sent home to Southern Ireland.'

He said nothing more and so without discussing the subject further the ex-private and the ex-RSM went on to Leeds in silence where they shook hands and parted, he to Liverpool and the night boat to Eire and me, the ex-private, to Dewsbury.

It was a poignant farewell after our shared experiences during the previous nine months of war and I like to think the ex-RSM was at least seen off at the last moment by one of his ordinary KOYLIs who still respected him, regardless of the court verdict.

He was a good RSM, very smart, good for his men, good for morale and very good for discipline, even though he was a bit of a tyrant. He was a fine example to us all of what a RSM should be.

I went back to work the next day and became a 70-hours-a-week worker in munitions, 12 hours a day and 6 days a week for the next 12 months plus quite a few Sundays when there were rush jobs. I was involved in the making of jigs and tools for 8-in shells, tank gear boxes, hand grenade bodies and switchgear for fitting on the open decks of destroyers. On top of this was fire-watching for one night in five, it was slavery and no mistake. How I got out of that and back into the Army is another story.

My time in the Army was never easy but was always worthwhile and something I shall always be proud of.

Diary of Events

I THINK IT WOULD BE an advantage to readers if I include a diary comparing my movements and incidents which concerned me with the greater events of the War and, perhaps more importantly, with movements of the German Army in my vicinity as near as I can ascertain them.

It is written on a daily basis for the duration of my time in the 1940 campaign in France, including my return home, beginning with the main German attack starting on 10 May.

Friday, 10 May 1940

German forces attacked Fort Eban Emael at dawn. This was a modern fort on the Belgian frontier with Germany and the initial attack was by glider-borne troops. A desperate struggle ensued but it didn't take long for these elite, well-rehearsed German troops, reinforced by paratroops, and using newly developed pipe bombs and flame-throwers, to overcome the Belgian defenders of this key fortification, even though the Belgians fought to the death.

German aircraft also attacked BEF HQ at Arras and military air bases throughout northern France and the Low Countries.

Three Dutch airfields were taken over by German paratroops in the first few hours. Fighters strafed The Hague, the centre of Rotterdam was destroyed and other city centres attacked as a warning to the Dutch.

Allied forces took up their positions on the Dyle-lower Meuse line as planned months earlier, leaving their well-dug-in positions on the Franco/Belgian frontier.

General Ironside, BEF Commander, wrote 'A long battle is going to ensue, and on the whole the advantage is with us.'

Sunday, 12 May 1940

BEF formations had taken up their positions on the Dyle in Belgium. German armoured formations reach the River Meuse far upstream in the evening, near Sedan, moving from inside Germany and across Luxemburg, with the Allies seemingly unaware of these moves until they hit the Meuse and begin crossing it using the existing bridges, portable bridges and assault boats.

Monday, 13 May 1940

Very heavy bombing by most of the Luftwaffe directed at a narrow front of the Meuse/Sedan area and its approaches. German engineer units repairing bridges damaged by Allies, but not destroyed, and also building new portable bridges across the Meuse near Sedan.

Tuesday, 14 May 1940

Allied Air Forces try to destroy these bridges but fail with very heavy losses, believed to average 50 per cent, i.e. 170 bombers set off on one raid and only 85 returned with many of these damaged. French Commander-in-Chief said 'Destroy these bridges or we are lost', and he was right.

By noon, German armour, backed up by associated infantry in armoured personnel carriers, with artillery and the maximum force of the Luftwaffe striking ahead of them, was pouring across the river bridges to smash at the junction of the French Second and Ninth armies.

Ironside was still convinced the main German attack would be made on the BEF and not on the French at the Meuse, little realising the BEF were soon to be one of the subjects of a gigantic pincer attack starting from the Meuse and swinging up through the Somme valley near Amiens and Abbeville to Boulogne and Calais and back eastwards towards Belgium. A kind of left hook by a super heavy-weight!

Meanwhile the BEF were temporarily spared serious fighting and so could not visualise the power of the enemy or the nature of the threat that was building up away on the Meuse, far away to the south.

Churchill and the War Cabinet in London also believed the main attack was to be through Belgium and, because the BEF was having a relatively mild time for the moment, could not believe French stories of catastrophe at Sedan and on the Meuse.

Wednesday, 15 May 1940

After five days of violent fighting and the exemplary bombing of the centres of numerous large cities in Holland, including Rotterdam, Holland was compelled to surrender to Germany. Their army, though small, was still fighting desperately right up to the last moment.

French Prime Minister, cognisant of events unfolding at Sedan and on the River Meuse, phoned Churchill to say, 'We are beaten – we have lost the battle.'

Churchill found this incredible, unbelievable in fact, yet events were soon to prove that it was true.

Thursday, 16 May 1940

BEF and French forces begin forced withdrawals in Belgium, moving back towards the Senne canals on their way back in a 60-mile major withdrawal to a new defensive line based on the River Escaut. This withdrawal took place in some confusion, however, particularly in respect of transport for British armoured vehicles.

Friday, 17 May 1940

German forces had created a complete breakthrough on the River

Meuse near Sedan where the French Second Army joined the French Ninth Army, the latter being something of a reserve force not equipped for the Blitzkrieg warfare it had faced. It was said that the German forces for this attack comprised in total about forty-four divisions, all either armoured or motorised, and that they were formed up in three columns stretching well back over 100 miles from the start point into Germany. This force was in fact nearly twice the size of the German Army Group attacking the combined BEF, the French First Army, the Belgians and the Dutch in the north.

Ian Hay, in his narrative *The Battle of Flanders* speaks of the situation on the Meuse being 'obscure' and no doubt it was with the enemy strength increasing to more than ten Panzer divisions plus supporting motorised infantry, artillery, supplies and about 2,000 tactical aircraft, all commanded by Panzer generals of the calibre of von Runstedt, Guderian and Rommel.

By now there was a feeling of alarm spreading through the Allied armies with further withdrawals being necessary.

However, reinforcements were beginning to move towards the east and north from the west, including us, the 2/4th KOYLI, who were now packing our bags in the camp near Rennes. Better late than never, one could say.

Saturday, 18 May 1940

Today, 2/4th KOYLI moved off by train to Rouen and the east.

German forces now nearing Amiens, the city to which we were heading in order to cross the Somme water barriers by train, though we did not know this.

Sunday, 19 May 1940

2/4th KOYLI arrived at Rouen in the evening, meanwhile the van of the German Panzer Army was passing Amiens heading north-west for Boulogne, Calais and Dunkirk, after what was really a rout of the unfortunate French Ninth Army in the area west of Sedan.

Monday, 20 May 1940

2/4th KOYLI passed by Dieppe and moved on to near Abbeville where in the late evening we were very heavily bombed with most of our equipment destroyed. Also smashed up were other units in our division, such as the Duke of Wellington's Regiment.

Meanwhile, the German Panzer Army was moving past Amiens and towards the back of Abbeville while the remnants of 2/4th KOYLI, which included me, were reforming north of Abbeville ready to move forward in a vain effort to get up to the main BEF to the north-east.

Preliminary planning for the evacuation of the BEF was put in hand by Admiral Ramsay.

Tuesday, 21 May 1940

Gort, Commander-in-Chief of the BEF, had been ordered by London to put up more fight, so a scratch force had been created to head south of Arras in conjunction with the French to join up with French forces striking from the south, i.e. the Gamelin plan, now called the Weygand plan, to cut off the German armoured spearhead. It was too late, however, probably nearly a week too late and had no chance of success. The BEF were outgunned and outnumbered but this small Allied semi-blitzkrieg tank clash gave the first German divisions they came across a heavy beating, their first.

The elite SS division 'Totenkopf' panicked somewhat but other German Panzers rescued them and the surviving BEF tank units were forced to retreat.

One of my friends was among the many captured here and was a prisoner for five years.

Despite the above limited success, the Anglo/French penetrations could not be held and so the railway through Abbeville was now cut and all links between north and south across the Somme waterways were broken.

Meanwhile, we, the small remnant of 2/4th KOYLI, were moving off from the fields at the back of Abbeville, where we had spent the night, towards the north-east. I, and a few others of the regimental Intelligence Section, went forward on foot with Lieutenant Lee to observe the enemy along our line of march. Reporting back to our HQ, our temporary commander, Captain Keeping, realising the hopelessness of our position, decided to share out our very limited food rations prior to us moving back independently in small groups towards the Dieppe area where it was believed our division was to be reformed.

Later in the day I, and my small group, shot up a reconnaissance party of German motorcyclists who came on us without warning at a time when we were sat down on a wall having a bite to eat. But our weapons were loaded and pointing in their direction so they were unlucky. We seemed to shoot without thinking, and it was all over in seconds. It was our first certain kill.

Late in the evening, I, who seemed by now to have lost my mates somehow, was on the receiving end of a most violent air raid on Abbeville. So far as I was concerned, the 2/4th KOYLI was now completely scattered and I was alone among refugees, civilian and military, numbering tens of thousands. I wandered with them, going where they went, without either leadership or direction from anyone.

Wednesday, 22 May 1940

After a lost twenty hours or so, during which time I had no recollection of where I was or what had happened, I found myself walking along a road near the coast heading west.

I was making for Dieppe, away from Abbeville. It was getting dark as I remember it.

I was stopped at an Army road block and with others put into a defensive line being formed. I was given the job of manning a Vickers machine-gun. It was dark and we were now awaiting an expected German attack.

The ports of Boulogne and Calais were now being overrun and I would think some of the German Panzers were being redirected towards Normandy as a preliminary to bringing the main weight of their armour round the west of Paris, so cutting the French forces in half, i.e. now a right hook by this super heavyweight!

Thursday, 23 May 1940

The BEF as a whole was put on half rations. I of course was now on zero rations and had been for some days, though unexpectedly I did get one good meal and a gill of army rum while I was manning the machine-gun.

I was in action against German infantry making probing attacks which developed into full-scale local engagements with Stukas, tanks, mortars and infantry against our infantry and heavy AA guns.

British troops, including me, withdrawn during the night and our places taken over by the French Army. We continued our withdrawal towards Dieppe.

Panzers attacking west in Abbeville/Amiens sector, making probing attacks to assess the strength of the Allies in this area of future decisive action.

Friday, 24 May 1940

Reached Eu, mostly by walking but got a lift on a train. Was involved in trains being bombed and a civilian train wreck. Had my first real meal in a sort of rough cafeteria at the Eu depot.

Saturday, 25 May 1940

Recuperate at Eu depot. Seemed a quiet time. While looking round the place I met more stragglers limping in and to my amazement there was my old mate Geoff Grimshaw among them whom I hadn't seen since we left Rennes. He looked absolutely done in. Sorted him out, got him a bed and decided to stay until tomorrow with him.

Sunday, 26 May 1940

On our way out of this depot and on our way to Dieppe. Suffered more bombing, strafing and at night shot up an unknown tracked vehicle. During night it rained and as I felt Geoff must get a lift I held up a Belgian car and made him take us to Dieppe. No sleep this night.

Monday, 27 May 1940

Walked into Dieppe expecting to find British Army in full control of defensive positions – but there was nothing there, it was a dead town, absolutely dead. Found an abandoned motorbike down near docks so we got it going and set off for Rouen. I was absolutely sure we would meet British formations during our journey to Rouen but we met no one and then about 20 miles down the road we ran out of petrol.

Stayed night in an emergency dormitory and soup kitchen being run by International Red Cross and decided to wait a few days in hopes of getting petrol as Geoff still wasn't in too good a shape to start walking the 60-odd miles to Rouen.

Tuesday, 28 May 1940

An English language teacher from the local Lycee heard of our plight and took us in for a few nights. He fed us and let us sleep on thick feather beds and used his influence to get us five litres of petrol when a black market tanker came in.

Wednesday, 29 May 1940

Still at teacher's house.

Thursday, 30 May 1940

Still at teacher's house but beginning to worry about lack of petrol and at our predicament, waiting and waiting, with the enemy getting nearer every day.

Friday, 31 May 1940

Petrol came at last and as promised we got five precious litres for five pounds sterling and set off for Rouen which we reached in the evening. At last we had caught up with the British Army complete with redcaps who directed Geoff to the motor pool and me to a meal and bed space in an enormous British army base camp.

I lost Geoff after we separated and didn't see him again in France.

Saturday, 1 June 1940

The Glorious 1st of June! But no sign of Geoff and no men from 2/4th KOYLI Where is everybody?

I waited and waited and searched and searched everywhere I could reach on foot, but no one wanted me, in some ways it was a madhouse, there did not seem to be any control or direction. Meanwhile the ongoing Dunkirk evacuation was drawing to a close and though we didn't know it at the time we down here would soon be on our own. The French with a few British units, including the 51st Highland Division and part of an armoured division, would fight on in the approaches to Rouen and its bridges over the River Seine.

Sunday, 2 June 1940

Got a job doing guard duty in Rouen city centre. At least it was something useful.

Monday, 3 June 1940

Guard duty.

Tuesday, 4 June 1940

Guard duty, again. Though we didn't know it, today was the end of the Dunkirk evacuation.

Wednesday, 5 June 1940

Violent air raids on camp, dreadful raids on us personally. German offensive began at 0400 hrs across the River Somme to our north-east, towards lower Seine below Paris, by Army Group B under von Bock. Said to be with over 600 tanks along a 6 km front in the van with many more behind them as 'back-up'.

Thursday, 6 June 1940

Air raids continue, causing immense damage in camp and to strategic targets nearby. I, with others, were manning AA defences and surviving by the skin of our teeth.

Friday, 7 June 1940

Rommel 80 km from Rouen at dawn but during day advanced 40 km. I continued to man AA defences on the base.

Saturday, 8 June 1940

Rommel moving right up to the Seine where it curves like a thumb a few miles up-river from Rouen, near where our camp was – but we were on the safer left-bank side of the river.

This day I had my trade test with the RASC mobile workshop, and then worked like a slave repairing the big trucks damaged by the bombing.

After more air raids we moved to the south-west; at least I now had a unit to which I belonged, temporarily.

Sunday, 9 June 1940

Rommel took Rouen and Elbeuf after heavy fighting round the city.

We were now at Bourgtheroulde for the night, near Rouen, but to the south-west.

Monday, 10 June 1940

Moved to Bernay, 20 miles or so of chaos on the roads. Took all day.

Tuesday, 11 June 1940

We were ordered down to Argantan and I get job of guard on bus full of French girls who were also going to Argantan.

Italy declared war on France but they got a bloody nose from Alpine troops and Foreign Legion in the Mediterranean approaches to France.

Wednesday, 12 June 1940

Saw reinforcements for British Army moving east through Argantan early in the morning – Canadians, who had a lot to say about us going west. A lot of sarcasm!

Late in the evening we saw these same Canadians moving back west and this time they had nothing to say.

Today the 51st Highland Division with remnants of the French IX Corps were forced to surrender at St Valery, west of Dieppe, at 0800 hrs in the morning. They had no choice as the small port where most of them were was ringed by the guns of 7th Panzer Division plus much heavy artillery. For them there was no escape.

Thursday, 13 June 1940

We moved to Alencon via Sees.

Friday, 14 June 1940

We moved a bit more to the west, the town of Laval comes to mind, but getting confused now. Also becoming very short of food and cigarettes, the latter being the more important.

Saturday, 15 June 1940

Late at night arrived at a big semi-abandoned base near St Nazaire. Now we could get everything we wanted, cigs, food, uniforms, ammunition etc. and we went to bed happy for the first time in some days.

Meanwhile Germans marched into Paris and the Panzers raced after the Allied forces retreating to Cherbourg.

Sunday, 16 June 1940

Working at this supply depot smashing trucks. Today Premier Reynaud resigns and President Lebrun asks his Vice-President, Marshal Pétain, to form a government.

Monday, 17 June 1940

Fall of French Government which had been led by Reynaud.

Last British and Polish troops leave Cherbourg at 1830 hrs on *Duke of Athol.*

Panzers near Rennes and other columns near Tours.

About midnight, or just after, we were called on parade and set off marching down to the docks of St Nazaire some miles away to join the *Lancastria*, the big liner sent to rescue we survivors. It seemed a long way but we were quite cheerful at the thoughts of going home at last. I even think there was some singing as we marched those last miles to the quays.

We eventually got there just in time to be met by another massive air raid. It was still dark. I got hit in the knee and the earlier singing began to seem a bit premature!

Some confusion during the rest of the night as we found there was no *Lancastria*, it had sailed without us.

More confusion this day because of the bombing and its consequences and the sailing of the *Lancastria*.

And I think I was shell-shocked again as I seem to have no real memory of events at this very critical time for us.

Tuesday, 18 June 1940

We hear of de Gaulle fleeing to England sometime yesterday from a French civilian and also of Marshal Pétain being made Head of State. There are stories too of negotiations for an armistice, or a ceasefire.

Panzers entered Rennes and the other column coming our way neared Nantes.

Wednesday, 19 June 1940

We left St Nazaire on trucks taken from the base after victualling them with cigs, food, petrol, weapons and ammunition sufficient for a run of several hundred miles – as we didn't know where we were going to end up, though we thought it might be northern Spain or Portugal.

So it was another Robinson Crusoe job! We moved south, crossed the Loire river just ahead of the Panzers who took Nantes today, and came to a small harbour with a single quay where we found a small ship tied up embarking troops such as we.

Episode of the Jews, we sailed at dusk, due west as far as we could judge.

Thursday, 20 June 1940

Sailed west with Lewis guns permanently manned. Panzers took Vichy.

Friday, 21 June 1940

Sailed west, AA guard relaxed a bit now we were moving out of range of shore-based aircraft.

French Government received German Armistice terms at Compiègne.

Saturday, 22 June 1940

Continued sailing west. Rumours that we were going to America or Canada. Turned north in late afternoon.

Sunday, 23 June 1940

Sailed north until midday, then turned east. We knew now we were not going to America!

Monday, 24 June 1940

Sailing east all day. Maginot Line ordered to surrender at 0035 hrs 25 June.

Tuesday, 25 June 1940

Arrived Plymouth in morning, marched up to station for train to Mansfield, receiving a tumultuous reception from enormous crowds including thousands of women seeking their missing menfolk as we were supposed to be the last boat from France.

Arrived Mansfield, marched through town to a barracks for a few nights.

Ceasefire in France came into effect at 1235 hrs on 25 June. Panzers reached Royan, Angoulême and Bordeaux. War over on European mainland.

Wednesday, 26 June 1940

Security screening, I surrendered my Bren to armoury.

Thursday, 27 June 1940

Discussed my future with recruiters from the Paras and Leopards, I didn't fancy Paras so I decide to join Leopards.

Panzers reached Spanish frontier so if we had gone on into Spain at Hendaye, as we were thinking of doing, we would have made it ahead of them.

Friday, 28 June 1940

By train to Sheffield in late afternoon. Sold some cigarettes to get some cash as the one pound the Army gave me at Mansfield was spent – these were the days when one could buy a fish and chip supper, a pint of beer and go home on the bus and still have change out of 5p. Or is it 5 pee?

Saturday, 29 June 1940

Sent home to Dewsbury for 48-hour leave – home at last! It was my birthday – I was 20 that day and I still didn't know who won the War. But I was in one piece, thank God.

August (sometime) 1940

I was released by the Army on Class A Reserve to go back to work temporarily on munitions.

Epilogue

I NOW COME to a most difficult part of this story, as I must try to draw some sensible and valid conclusions from these events. The first thing to emphasise, most strongly, is that all I write actually occurred. I have not exaggerated anything; where I have deviated from the raw truth at all it is only in very minor ways and done to minimise the impact of events, i.e. to play it down somewhat as I did not want to produce a blood and guts Hollywood story. In those areas where I had no clear memory of things I say so, I do not try to invent.

I have said something about the reception we got on our return to England – the only people who seemed aware of events after Dunkirk seemed to be those who had lost someone over there. There was a feeling of almost shame in the general population because we had been defeated, as if they didn't want to know about those who had been left behind or those in the second BEF who were sent over there to help France. All they wanted to hear about were stories of the miracle of the Dunkirk evacuation. Nothing else seemed to matter.

There was also a deep feeling of resentment against France because of the defeat. There was no conception of what it means to a country when nearly a fifth of the population is uprooted from their homes and forced onto the roads as refugees by enemy action. And then to keep them moving they are repeatedly shot up and harassed by enemy fighter planes.

What would it be like in England if the whole of the population of Kent, East and West Sussex and all London's people south of the Thames were driven off towards East Anglia, Oxford and Swindon by unstoppable German Panzer divisions?

These Panzers, in this scenario, would be rapidly advancing north and west after successfully crossing the Channel and landing half a million men between Ramsgate and Eastbourne while the Home Army would have suffered a million casualties trying to stop them.

Ask yourself – what would it be like?

And when these wretched civilian refugees have reached what they think is relative safety, they and their hosts are driven on yet again by the still advancing enemy who in about four weeks overrun all the SE of England, plus London and the country up to the outskirts of Birmingham.

Do they know, or even do they care, what this means to a modern fairly compact country like France or Britain?

And then there is the bravery, or foolhardiness, of some of the men I met. Such as the soldier at Rouen who rushed to man the four-barrelled AA pom-pom to fire at the approaching German fighter aircraft shooting up the base. Or the men I was with, both British and French, who manned the ridge west of the Somme canal and stopped, albeit only temporarily, the German advance. Maybe it was a stop of only a few hours but it perhaps gave someone further back the chance to escape, or avoid serious trouble. Or the Royal Engineers in the sewers under the main streets of Amiens who rolled bundles of dynamite under German tanks as they advanced up the streets. Why did they do that? I could go on a long time in this vein but I've given you the picture.

Another point I must make, and it is very important to me, is the overriding importance of the pre-war regimental system of recruiting based on an area or a district, such as our KOYLI battalion based on a very small area of West Yorkshire in which companies, e.g. HQ Company, would be recruited in the main from a small locality like

Dewsbury. Thus the members of that company had a common upbringing of town, school and church. The result of knowing each other's background, family and friends was to tighten the regimental bonds of loyalty, comradeship and mutual support. This would take months to achieve in units recruited from strangers coming from a wider area.

One result of this was to make crimes such as cowardice, serious assault and insubordination more damning and damnable by its effect on the local people in the area from which the men were recruited.

Which is why it was so shocking for me to lose my mates after Abbeville, and to see some of them again for only a few moments on the hay cart near Rouen was such a delight. Then to lose them completely after that sighting and never see them again was a real loss.

Now, in 2000, I am led to believe that this type of recruitment is being abandoned in the name of efficiency.

Having said all this, and some of my remarks will not be well received by everyone, I should state unequivocally that as a result of what I saw and heard in this war, I am now wholly in favour of the European Common Market. Despite all its alleged restrictions on so-called National Sovereignty, it is the only way to prevent war in the future. Wars only get worse, never better, as we have witnessed in the Yugoslavian civil war. When some politician tries to tell you different, look what it is that this snake oil salesman is trying to sell – and don't buy it no matter what his label says.

The other big thing to come out of the War for me is the feeling that there is something out there beyond our understanding, beyond our tiny world with all its faults, which is trying to keep us on a path by which we will come to understand eventually what it is all about. I say this because of the many, many near squeaks with eternity I had in my life in 1940 and after.

A young woman whom I met in France in 1993, when I was on

a coach trip to Rennes le Chateau, north-west of Perpignan, summed it all up when she said to me, 'Someone up there is looking after you, you must have something more to do in this world before you go.'

This followed my telling her that I had suffered very severe septicaemia the previous year, with a temperature rising up to desperate levels, yet I had recovered and was now down here seeing this special tiny church with its strange history.

I have never forgotten that remark. So I say again, do not let the snake oil salesmen, who exist everywhere, in the church as well as in politics, lead you astray. Your religious beliefs are between you and your God and do not let anyone come between you if it looks as if that might happen.

May the spirit be with you, regardless of what you call it.

Bibliography

Amouroux, Henri, *La vie des francais sous l'occupation.*

Churchill, Winston S., *The Second World War*, Vol. 3 'The Fall of France'.

Duteurtre, Maurice, 'Les Amys du Vieux Dieppe', a letter from the President of 'Les Amys du Vieux Dieppe', which confirms my dates of events at Dieppe affecting Geoff Grimshaw and myself.

Forty, George and Duncan, John, *The Fall of France. Disaster in the West 1939–40.*

Gelb, Norman, 'DUNKIRK, The Incredible Escape', *Readers Digest.*

Guderian, General Heinz, *Panzer Leader*, chapter 5.

Hay, Ian, *The Battle of Flanders 1940*, HMSO.

Historical Association Studies, *Occupied France – Collaboration and Resistance 1940–1944.*

Hogg, Ian V., *The Encyclopedia Of Infantry Weapons Of World War II.*

Liddel Hart, B.H. (ed.), *The Rommel Papers*, Part I, 'France 1940'.

Nobecourt, R.G., *Les Soldats de 40 dans la premiere Bataille de Normandie.*

Public Record Office Kew, who kindly allowed me to see the secret war diaries of 2/4th Battalion KOYLI covering the period April–June 1940. Information in these papers is censored for 100 years, until July 2040, and therefore I have not used it in this story, although it was naturally encouraging to realise War Diary dates agreed with my own memories and the dates given me by French sources.

My own memories of these events round which this story is written, together with conversations I had with my comrade, Geoff Grimshaw, about our time in the Army together. Unfortunately Geoff is now deceased and so cannot join with me in this story.

Appendix I

The Bren Light Machine-Gun

I SHOULD GIVE SOME information on the Bren gun to which I refer so often. It was a light machine-gun, designed in Czechoslovakia in the early 1930s, The design may have been influenced to some extent by the French Chatellerault gun, though the latter was probably not a good influence as it had a disastrous record during its early years of service in France.

The Bren Mark I as I knew it was a beautiful pre-war designed gun, later models were heavier, uglier and cheaper. The Mark I had a ratchet-operated drum-type rear sight, a telescopic front bipod support, a folding cocking handle and various lightening grooves and cut-outs on the body. It weighed just over 20 lb which though heavy enough could be carried over the shoulder with its shoulder strap without too much trouble. I only found one fault with it, the barrel would get hot very quickly and you had to be always changing barrels during prolonged firing to enable them to cool off. You had a spare, of course, but when it was not convenient to change the barrel you had to beware of the hot one on the gun or else you'd get a bad burn, and that could happen at a most awkward moment.

It had a sustained rate of fire of about 500 rounds per minute but with a magazine capacity of only thirty rounds you would never fire non-stop at that rate. It also dramatically lost accuracy when fired in bursts longer than three or four rounds. But in short bursts it was as accurate as a rifle in my experience and could even be fired from the hip in short bursts with accuracy at ranges up to 100 yards. Using tracer bullets I have fired from the hip into a bedroom window

Bren gunner in training with a loader assisting. He is using a MKI Bren of 1938–39 (Imperial War Museum F3594)

at 100 yards range and seen most of the tracers go streaking through the window from burst after burst. It was like tossing tennis balls into a bucket at a fair! In this respect it was much better than a Thompson sub-machine-gun, though it hadn't got the hitting power of the latter at short range.

Without doubt, the Bren was one of the finest light machine-guns ever made. Gas operated, its mechanical components were simple and easily understood. It could be stripped and reassembled by a trained soldier in a very short time. There were only a few possible stoppages, and the Bren built up an enviable reputation for accuracy and reliability during the Second World War.

Appendix II

Answers to Questions Put by my Family

A NUMBER OF QUESTIONS have been put to me by members of my family whom I have asked to read the draft of this story as the various chapters have appeared.

I think it would be useful to record these with my comments as they are questions which may interest other readers.

Question 1: 'Who tells you where to go when you are alone?'

The answer to that is that you are under an obligation to try to obey the last order you have been given, always assuming the last order is a sensible and rational order and that it can be carried out. Thus when we were ordered to make for the Dieppe area, some 60 or 70 miles away, it was possible to obey it.

Question 2: 'Where do you get your food from, your water and your general supplies?'

My answer to that is simple – you get them where you can which may be from British sources, or from the land or from civilian sources, but within reason you must get food and water in order to continue with your duties. In other words you steal it if you have to, there is no alternative, but you do not steal it from people whose needs are greater than yours or from your own mates. Supplies are a different proposition, e.g. ammunition or weapons. You get them from army stores, but failing that if you overrun a depot or a supply dump you simply help yourself to whatever you need.

Question 3: 'Did you think of taking jewellery or money from the dead civilians on the train wreck you came across?'

No, and quite honestly the thought of doing that never entered my head. They were dead and that was that.

However, I took the bottles of champagne I found and some sandwiches from the wreckage of the bar without a qualm; they were simply immediate food and drink to me and I was not then to know I was soon to be in an abandoned supply dump where everything was available.

Question 4: 'Why did you steal the civilian motorbike in Dieppe?'

Because it was believed to be a matter of life or death that Geoff and I got out of that dead town and across the River Seine before we got cut off by the Germans. The Seine was far away to the south and we were sure we would not make it by walking, so some means of transport was essential. The owner was believed by us to be dead and we were pretty sure the bike would eventually reach his family if we took it as we were only borrowing it, not stealing it. So, rightly or wrongly, we took it and surrendered it to the authorities eventually in Rouen.

Question 5: 'How did you get money?'

I didn't get any money during the time I was on the road. We were paid at the beginning, about 9 or 10 May, and that was it so far as the Army were concerned. I had a fiver sewn in my uniform and I earned some more money by my semi-civilian guard duties.

Question 6: 'Don't you think it was foolhardy to set the rum wagons on fire at St Nazaire?'

No, not really. The men in the trucks fighting for the rum were in a dangerous mood, they were drunk and they were armed. It was a bad combination and if we could scatter them without being detected it was a good move. The alternative involved a risk of physical violence, even shooting. The resulting fire on the ammunition train was unexpected but of no consequence really as we were trying to destroy the base anyway.

Question 7: 'Don't you think you were a bit trigger happy, shooting at an unknown tracked vehicle in the dark near Eu, shooting after a car and shooting at a tank at St Nazaire?'

No I don't think so. In such circumstances I think it is better to shoot first and shoot at full power; no shooting to miss or to frighten. The exception was the car where I deliberately shot to miss but frighten.

Question 8: 'You seem to have been on an endless retreat all the way from Abbeville to St Nazaire where you caught a boat for home. Surely there was more in it than that for a whole battalion?'

Yes, of course there was. So far as we, the ordinary soldiers, were concerned we had no plans of our own. We simply existed on a day-to-day basis hoping to be fed sometime, having somewhere dry to sleep and be kept supplied with weapons and ammunition. Orders were few and far between.

We were told to rendezvous north-east of Abbeville, then to get down the coast to the west near Dieppe to join up with more British troops where new positions were being made. Later, when I got to Rouen, circumstances made me temporarily attach myself to a suitable motorised unit.

After that I simply went where they went, generally not knowing where we were going. That's all there was to it for me, no maps, no plan, just keep going and try to obey the last order.

Abbreviations

AA	Anti-aircraft
BEF	British Expeditionary Force
CSM	Company Sergeant Major
HQ	Headquarters
KOYLI	King's Own Yorkshire Light Infantry
LMG	Light machine-gun
NCO	Non commissioned officer
OC	Officer Commanding
OCTU	Officer Cadet Training Centre
QM	Quartermaster
RAOC	Royal Army Ordnance Corps
RASC	Royal Army Service Corps
REME	Royal Electrical and Mechanical Engineers
RQMS	Regimental Quartermaster Sergeant
RSM	Regimental Sergeant Major
RTO	Railway Traffic Officer